NASTY NEIGHBORS:

A GUIDE TO DEALING WITH DISRUPTIVE AND DIFFICULT NEIGHBORS

Patrick MacQueen, Esq.

ISBN 978-0-578-73544-3

To Jennifer, Liam, and Rory,
my 3 reasons for constantly striving to be better.

———◆———

To the memory of Laurence W. MacQueen, PhD,
who was never able to finish his book.

Table of Contents

PREFACE

The Bible tells us to love our neighbors, and also to love our enemies; probably because generally they are the same people.

— *G.K. Chesterton*

I was meeting with the Johnstones at 11am on a Thursday morning. The Johnstones, as I later discovered, were a middle-aged, working class couple living in a HOA-free suburb of Phoenix. Mrs. Johnstone was a school teacher, and Mr. Johnstone was a welder. They were annoyingly early for their meeting, but I'd later discover that their promptness was for good reason. They needed a solution to their problem with Bernie, and they needed it fast.

As I approached the conference room, I noticed through the partially-glazed window what appeared to be a husband and a wife, both shaking, and obviously upset. I quickly learned why: "Last night my neighbor spit in my husband's eye, and this morning we woke up to a middle finger painted on my neighbor's home with the words 'FUCK the Johnstones' painted above the middle finger." "What? Wait a minute", I replied, "Did you just say that your neighbor spit in your husband's face and then painted profanity on his own garage because he was mad at you?" At the time, I had previously consulted and dealt with clients whose own properties had been damaged by neighbors, neighbors involved in fist fights, and neighbors who intentionally damaged another neighbor's home, but until then I had never heard of neighbors doing terrible things to their own homes. "Yes!" Mrs. Johnstone yelled, and went on to tell me that she needed an immediate solution to deal with the man across the street, who, prior to this incident, had never shown any signs of dislike for her family.

I stepped away from this consultation shaking my head. I had never encountered someone like Bernie, who, as I later found out, parked a beat up pickup truck with grungy toilets in front of the Johnstones' home and had been video-taping the Johnstones' seventeen-year-old daughter, among other things. I thought I'd seen it all. Neighbors stealing water; neighbors taking land; constant loud music and partying; fictitious HOA "actions" to drive people out of their homes; and, now, Bernie.

It has been almost a year since my representation of the Johnstones ended. They moved away from a home they loved and Bernie paid for his transgressions, although his house is now painted in multiple bright colors. In that year, I have compiled a list of the most salacious and stupid things that neighbors have done, and continue to do, to one another. In addition to that list, I have also compiled a list of legal claims that one can make against an obnoxious neighbor like Bernie.

My greatest fear is that one of my clients, and the Bernie living next door to them, would turn into a news story about something horrific happening at one of their homes.

Like, for example, the neighbor who went nuts over the size of his next door neighbor's newly constructed wall and decided to rent a bulldozer and plow through his neighborhood, destroying the wall, and knocking down his own garage (by accident). Or, the neighbor who was sick of the loud music and partying by short term renters at the home next to his and decided to take the law into his own hands by breaking the pipes at the home and flooding out the party. Or, the fed up neighbor who is now on probation for beating his neighbor with a shovel. Apparently, the victim failed to replace a boundary fence in a timely fashion and, after weeks of obnoxious text messages between the neighbors, one man took a gardening tool to the other's head. Or, the neighbor who accidentally cemented over his neighbor's drainage ditch causing fairly minor flooding. He was ultimately shot for his mistake.

As for the Johnstones and Bernie, they did make the news. Fortunately, they made the news because of the public debate surrounding whether the local municipality should step in and require that Bernie stop spray painting profane words on his home. As it turned out, the municipality chickened out as there was concern that Bernie would turn things into a claim that the municipality infringed on his right of free speech and artistic expression. As private citizens, the Johnstones had no such risk.

WHY THIS BOOK?

*"The neighbors always leave their sprinklers on,
which is a little bit annoying. It's a source of constant
irrigation."*

— *LaffGaff.com*

This book is designed to be a tool for the analysis, and possible resolution, of real estate issues and conflicts concerning neighbors and a guide to those affected by the Bernies of the world. This book should be useful for those with little experience in the area of real estate law and for those wanting help in everyday legal and practical real estate problems involving neighbors.

Whether you are dealing with an angry neighbor who has spray painted a middle finger on his own home because he doesn't like you, or you are fuming over your neighbors flying a drone directly above your pool to get a glimpse of your sunbathing girlfriend, this book is for you.

Throughout this book, we explore a range of examples of real neighbors and the very real legal principles that operate to define their rights and obligations. I will give you the tools to legally address common neighborhood problems, such as nuisance, trespass, easements, covenants, deed restrictions, adverse possession, and water rights. And, I provide pro tips for managing the newer areas of neighborhood conflict, such as homeowners' associations, and other less traditional issues, like the booming short term rental industry and its effect on neighbors. You'll also learn how our archaic and outdated rules shape and circumscribe the so-called rights of homeowners.

This book is organized in several parts with short stories about real life events. Each of the stories are followed by an explanation of the laws governing the characters in the story. If you do not want to read about Bernie the Toilet Collector and prefer to skip ahead to well share agreements, you can do that. None of the stories or explanations require reading the preceding sections before moving ahead. For example, you do not need to read about boundary disputes in Chapter 2 before reviewing the laws associated with short term rentals, addressed in Chapter 5.

The source and origin of our real estate laws are addressed first. We will then dig into the various types of agreements that neighbors can execute between themselves to govern the use of their properties. Next, while our wrongful lien and quiet title statutes originate from common law principles, many have now been codified and are addressed in the section relating to the statutory regulations of neighboring properties. Special types of neighbor issues, like homeowners' associations and short term rentals, are addressed last.

WARNING: THIS BOOK IS NOT REAL ESTATE OR LEGAL ADVICE

"He who represents himself has a fool for a client"
— Abe Lincoln

Most books come with a disclaimer. So, here is mine. This book provides legal information written on a legal topic with anecdotes from real life legal situations and is written by someone with legal experience and a law degree. But, it is not legal advice! The information provided in this book is of a general nature and may not be the most recent due to the volatile nature of statutes, rules, and cases.

Let me explain: I stand behind everything written in this book. However, the old cliché that every case is different applies here. Every specific set of facts calls for different analysis. Various factors and other moving parts are usually endless and, changing one small factor can, believe it or not, change the strategy or analysis entirely. As you will learn in this book, real estate laws have existed for centuries, and it is possible that a new statute or case becomes the law between the time I wrote this book and the time you read it. Taking this into consideration, you should not make decisions to sue your neighbor, cut down your neighbor's tree, paint a middle finger on your garage to piss off your neighbor, or create a stir at your next HOA meeting based on this book alone. And, it also goes without saying that this book does not create an attorney-client relationship.

CHAPTER ONE

The Origin And Sources Of Real Estate Laws

"Land monopoly is not only monopoly, but it is by far the greatest of monopolies; it is a perpetual monopoly, and it is the mother of all other forms of monopoly."

— Winston Churchill

The ownership of real estate, its sale, development, and disposition, represents a large chunk of the American economy, and residential real estate is often the largest financial investment most people ever make. Indeed, in 2018, real estate construction alone contributed $1.15 trillion to the Nation's economic output. The significance of protecting the rights of those who own real estate cannot be overstated. Interestingly enough, almost all real estate laws share a common legal beginning and history.

The predominant force behind our current real estate laws is largely attributed to William the Conqueror's Norman invasion of England in the 11th century. At the time, England was fractionalized as various groups, including Angles, Saxons, Celts, and Vikings, created settlements throughout the country. These distinct groups settled legal disputes differently and had their own legal customs. William the Conqueror's chief goal was to create one uniform "law" among all of England.

Under the "common law," legal issues were resolved on a case-by-case basis by judges in the King's court, called the Curia Regis. And, as English became the established language, the legal decisions of significance were written into books. The common law, or "judge-made" law, would be reviewed and referred to by subsequent judges in similar situations such that judges could utilize the case "precedence" to decide new cases.

In other words, when similar legal disputes arose, the judges had a way to refer back to earlier decisions as a basis to decide current cases. For better or worse, this decision making process, i.e., reviewing "earlier cases" is fully applied today.

The use of juries in deciding English cases can similarly be traced back to William the Conqueror (although portions of the jury system can trace back to the ancient Greeks). The English brought the jury system with them to the American colonies.

In addition to implementing the "common law," William the Conqueror largely created real property law. Under the system created by William the Conqueror, the King of England was the highest source of the law and all right to use land had to be traced to an authorization from the King. People were divided into "freeman" and "nonfreeman," which corresponded to the "freehold" and "nonfreehold" estates they owned in real estate. Only "freeman," who usually obtained their status based on bloodline, could own and hold title to real estate. In today's parlance, an owner of a freehold estate owns the title to real estate outright.

A nonfreeman in England could not own real estate. Rather, they could only own personal property, called chattels. A nonfreeman could only possess and occupy the real estate of another for a tenure – from which the word "tenant" was derived. Under the law as it currently exists, a nonfreehold estate consists of a landlord tenant relationship.

During America's colonial period, the colonies largely utilized the English common law system. And, to encourage colonization, the King of England granted to tenants the right to use land mostly for agricultural purposes. After the American Revolution, the United States allowed a tenant to acquire the real estate he previously occupied, and many of the concepts attributed to William the Conqueror still apply today.

Modern day real estate claims against neighbors, like those outlined in this book, have their origins in English common law. For instance, a claim of "nuisance" was one in which a defendant's actions "materially affect[ed] the reasonable comfort and convenience of life of a class of Her Majesty's subjects." As explained in this book, the elements of this claim, and others, are largely the same as they were when "her majesty's" subjects were the ones annoyed by their neighbors.

Cases

The cases cited throughout this text are "judge made" law, i.e., they are modern day interpretations of prior decisions and common law – i.e., the common law created a millennium ago.

Statutes

We also have another source for our real estate laws – the legislature. Statutes are laws that are passed by the legislature. For example, A.R.S. § 9-500.39 and A.R.S. § 11-269.17 are the statutes that prohibit cities, towns, and counties from prohibiting short term rentals, which, as addressed in Chapter 5, have been the source of numerous neighbor disputes. Another source of neighborhood drama is A.R.S. § 48-3613, which prohibits water diversion. Wait until you hear about the damage caused when this statute is violated.

CHAPTER TWO

Common Law Property Rights

"Good fences make good neighbors."

— Robert Frost

• Nuisance Laws and Bernie the Toilet Collector

John Babcock, a Korean war veteran, purchased a home for his daughter Wendy Johnstone, a local school teacher, and her family to live in. It was a modest home of approximately 1,900 square feet and it was perfect for the family. The neighborhood was quiet and close to everyone's work. Bernie owned the home directly across the Johnstones. Bernie originally purchased his home in the early 1980s and it was obvious he never updated it since his purchase.

Everything between the Johnstones and Bernie had been cordial, at least for the first 5 years after the Johnstones moved in. That changed sometime in 2016 when the Johnstones' daughter, Samantha, witnessed a heated altercation involving obscene gestures and vulgar language between Bernie and another neighbor, Frank. Samantha told her parents about the incident after returning home from school.

Later that week, disturbed by what his daughter witnessed, Steve Johnstone, Wendy's husband of nearly 20 years, walked over to Bernie's home to find out about what his daughter witnessed. Bernie refused to engage with Steve and told him that the altercation with the neighbor was "none of his fucking business."

The following morning the Johnstones awoke to find a large hand giving the middle finger painted on Bernie's garage door. The hand had been crudely drawn and it was obvious that it was directed at the Johnstones' home. Soon after Bernie painted the middle finger on his garage door, he posted "CAUTION" tape surrounding his property and a "KEEP OUT" sign near the front door. Bernie also started installing surveillance cameras to canvas the exterior of his home, and probably had 14 or so surveillance cameras on the exterior of his home pointed directly at the Johnstones' home and driveway.

About a week after the middle finger incident, someone attempted to paint over the artwork on Bernie's garage door and, of course, Steve was the prime suspect. He didn't do it, really.

About a week later, Bernie was caught taking pictures of Samantha without any reason as she was leaving her home for school – school, as in high school. On that same day, Bernie was caught openly taking pictures of other children in the neighborhood. This time it was neighbors' Saul and Sarah's young minor children – and, by young, we're talking toddlers. The police were called, and when an officer tried to speak with Bernie, he refused to answer the door. Good move, Bernie.

The following week, the Johnstones caught Bernie peeping over his side gate, taking pictures of the Johnstones as they installed their own surveillance cameras.

Completely creeped out over Bernie's bizarre behavior and his strange willingness to ruin his own garage over a heated discussion, a group of neighbors and Bernie met with city officials to have a "mediation" – i.e., a non-binding discussion - to try to cool things down a bit. At the mediation, Bernie agreed to paint over the latest edition of his middle finger painted on his garage if the neighbors agreed to leave him alone. That was no problem for any of the neighbors, as none of them wanted anything to do with Bernie. After the mediation, the Johnstones, and the other neighbors thought they had come to an agreement with Bernie; but, they were wrong. Bernie was just getting (re)started.

Just 2 days after the mediation, Bernie, through a "friend" he hired at a downtown art expo, graffitied the words "MENOPAUSE MANOR" on the wall above his garage, "OVERKILL" on the garage door, and "POUND SAND" next to the side gate. Bernie's art expo "friend" also graffitied an alien flipping the bird on the sidewall of his home. And, it got better.

About a week later, Bernie started parking an ice cream truck and an old ambulance on the street directly in front of his home and the Johnstones' home. Bernie parked these in the street, despite there being plenty of room in his driveway and two spaces in his garage. Bernie claimed that he purchased the ice-cream truck to pull a boat – one that he did not own and could not describe. He confirmed during his deposition that he had never owned a boat. And, he claimed to have purchased the ambulance for nostalgia purposes. Bernie was a firefighter in the mid-1980s and the ambulance brought back fond memories.

Bernie also started parking a pickup truck on the street in front of the Johnstones' home, its bed full of used, grungy toilets. He claimed to be a toilet collector and toilet broker, who, when called by someone with a toilet issue, would visit the caller's home and negotiate a deal on toilets. Imagine, someone without any experience in plumbing or with toilets, going house to house to discuss toilets. Yeah, right.

Not surprisingly, the Johnstones found surveillance cameras attached to the tailpipe of the ice cream truck pointing directly at their home, and would occasionally wave to it. The Johnstones later found a surveillance camera on the dashboard of the toilet-hauling pickup truck pointing directly at their home and, again, waved to Bernie every chance they had. They also discovered that Bernie labelled all of his Wi-Fi internet connections with the following titles: "FUCK YOU;" "FUCK YOU1;" "FUCK YOU2;" and "FUCK YOU3."

The Johnstones finally moved because of Bernie and his continued antics. Interestingly, once the Johnstones placed their home for sale and had their real estate agent place a "For Sale" sign in their front yard, Bernie actually removed his graffiti. Now, instead of graffiti, he painted the property in bright rainbow colors. Bernie was still not done being a nuisance, however.

A prospective buyer interested in purchasing the Johnstones' home as an investment entered into a real estate contract with the Johnstones. Ultimately, the buyer backed out of the contract due to Bernie. Apparently, Bernie approached the buyer and gave him a piece of his mind. Bernie informed the prospective purchaser that his antics would continue if the prospective purchaser chose to lease the home to tenants. According to Bernie, renters were "vermin" and ruined the neighborhood. The Johnstones were finally able to sell their home, albeit at a reduced price.

I always wondered what was wrong with Bernie and why he became so unhinged and why he decided to be so obnoxious. I also wondered what he had hidden in his home. Once I began questioning him about the interior of his home, which, not surprisingly was a basic off-white color (and not painted in rainbow colors or graffiti), he decided that settlement was in his best interest.

Since this is a chapter about nuisance laws and the many ways in which a neighbor's actions can constitute a nuisance, it goes without saying that Bernie's actions constituted a nuisance. There is more on nuisance later in this chapter.

Bernie also intruded upon the seclusion of the Johnstones, which is a property related issue that comes up every once in a while and has a history similar to that of nuisance. Intrusion upon seclusion occurs when someone, i.e., your neighborhood Bernie, intentionally intrudes, physically or otherwise, upon the solitude or seclusion of another or his private affairs or concerns. There is liability if the intrusion would be highly offensive to a reasonable person. When an intrusion occurs in a home, courts typically find the intrusion to be highly offensive to a reasonable person. Note: Bernie also interfered with a contract, which left him liable for the difference between the sales price of the initial contract and the second contract. Nice work, Bernie.

Nuisance law is an area of law divided into 2 parts. A "private" nuisance is one in which the actions of the defendant cause a substantial and unreasonable interference with a claimant's land or his/her use or enjoyment of that land. "Public" nuisance, on the other hand, is a situation in which the defendant's actions materially affect the comfort and convenience of citizens as part of the public (think of that noxious smelling dairy farm). Both types of nuisance claims have been present from the time of Henry III. Each claim of nuisance, whether private or public, requires the claimant to prove that the defendant's actions caused interference, which was unreasonable, and in some situations the intention of the defendant may also be taken into account. The concept of a nuisance originally came from the Latin nocumentum, and then the French nuisance, with Henry de Bracton initially defining the tort of nuisance as an infringement of easements. The claim was in line with the primary economic driver at the time of its creation – i.e., agriculture, and was used as a way of protecting claimants against a neighbors' right to develop.

By the 17th century the judicial philosophy had changed to allow the protection of a claimant's enjoyment of their land, with the duty being on the party that caused the nuisance to prevent it: "as every man is bound to look to his cattle, as to keep them out of his neighbour's ground; so he must keep in the filth of his house of office, that it may not flow in upon and damnify his neighbour".

Private nuisance was formally defined in Bamford v Turnley, where George Wilshere, 1st Baron of Bramwell defined it as "any continuous activity or state of affairs causing a substantial and unreasonable interference with a [claimant's] land or his use or enjoyment of that land". The definition remains largely the same now.

Under the current laws, a private nuisance claimant must first show that the defendant's actions have caused an interference with their use or enjoyment of the land. The interference must be substantial and it must constitute more than a slight inconvenience.

Judges like to say that they will not concern themselves with "trifles," and must see a real and appreciable invasion of someone's interests. And, ordinarily, there must be continuity or recurrence of an action over a period of time.

While there is no set definition of what constitutes "unreasonableness" a judge will consider various factors, including any "abnormal sensitivity" of the claimant, the nature of the locality where the nuisance took place, the time and duration of the interference and the conduct of the defendant.

Activities may be reasonable at one time but not at another; like in the case of the railstop in the middle of Gilbert, Arizona. Unloading freight at 10am was held to be reasonable, but the same activity undertaken at 10pm was unreasonable. Sometimes, the conduct of the defendant can be a factor in determining the unreasonableness of their interference. I have seen an instance in which a defendant deliberately created noise to anger his neighbors and, because of this, a judge found this conduct amounted to a nuisance.

A nuisance is "common" or "public" when it affects the rights which are enjoyed by citizens as a party of the public. The difference between a private nuisance and a public nuisance is generally one of degree. A private nuisance is one affecting a single individual or a small number of persons. To constitute a public nuisance, the nuisance must affect a considerable number or an entire community or neighborhood. Because of the broad definition of what constitutes a public nuisance, there are a large range of issues which can be dealt with through public nuisance, including blocking a waterway, dust, and noisy construction activities. The potential defendants in public nuisance claims are the same as those in private nuisance, with their liability dependent on a test of reasonableness; in public nuisance, however, this is determined by looking solely at the interference, not the defendant's actions.

Pro Tips: So what can you do when someone, or their dog, has become a nuisance? The first thing you should do is to try to speak your neighbor. Oftentimes, many people are just plain unaware that their dog barks incessantly during the day, or that their tenant likes to party at night. Once brought to their attention, you may see some results.

If your conversation does not go as planned, you'll want to start tracking things. Document the days the nuisance occurs and record what is going on. Call the police, if necessary, and obtain a copy of the police report. Once you have this information, send a "cease and desist" letter to your neighbor by certified mail. Here is an example:

SAMPLE LETTER

June 25, 2020

VIA FIRST CLASS MAIL AND CERTIFIED MAIL;
RETURN RECEIPT REQUEST TO:

_____

_____

_____

Re: Demand to Cease and Desist

Dear _____:

We understand you are the record owner of certain real property known as _____(the "Property"). As more fully described herein, the purpose of this letter is to demand you forever cease and desist from the nuisance created by your development of the Property.

As you are already likely aware, we own a neighboring property to you, as we presently hold title to the real property located at _____. ("Our Property"). Our Property is located at a lower elevation than Property. We have been a member of the community for approximately forty years, and, according to the official records of ____ County, Arizona, came into ownership of Our Property in or around June of 1997 via quitclaim deed.

While the ___County Assessor's Office indicates you first acquired title and ownership to the Property in or around April of 2018, in or around March of 2019 it appears you began developing the Property, including substantial excavation. Upon information and belief, you purchased the property as an investment opportunity to develop the land for residential purposes. While you may have obtained a basic building permit, no written consent or other specific permit was ever provided by the relevant board of ___ County to engage in the obstruction of a watercourse or to divert water onto Our Property.

As you may already be aware, the neighborhood is located within a major designated regulatory floodway, from which your Property and Our Property is located approximately only 350 feet. During our period of ownership and residence in the community, we have grown accustomed to the natural grading and water drainage patterns both on our Property and the immediate vicinity. During this time, our Property had never sustained a flooding event, including during some of the stronger monsoon seasons.

Recently, however, Our Property has received a substantial increase of rainfall water, which has been redirected from certain artificial developments located on your Property. While recent damage from the increased volume of water discharge has been minimal, this can largely be attributed to the minimal monsoon season, which has been widely reported as one of the driest of historical record. Future flooding events are anticipated to cause substantial flooding and damage to Our Property, including to the interior of the established residence.

Examination of the relevant parcels reveals the increased volume of water diversion is resulting from a large amount of vegetation removal and dirt/gravel relocation as incidental of the development of your Property. Arizona law prohibits such actions and gives rise to claims for (1) damages, (2) a temporary and permanent injunction; and (3) attorneys' fees and costs incurred in seeking your compliance.

Please allow this letter to confirm our unequivocal demand for you to cease and desist the current development and alterations causing the diversion of an increased flow of water onto our Property. Should you fail to immediately correct the natural drainage conditions of the neighboring areas to restore the watercourse to its original state, we intend to seek immediate affirmative relief and reimbursement of all costs and attorneys' fees by filing a formal complaint with the ___ County Superior Court.

Under Arizona law, a "trespasser" is one who does an unlawful act or a lawful act in an unlawful manner, causing injury of a person or another person's property. See MacNeil v. Perkins, 84 Ariz. 74, 82, 324 P.2d 211, 216 (1958). At

common law, any unauthorized physical presence on another's property was considered a trespass, State ex rel. Purcell v. Superior Court, 111 Ariz. 582, 584, 535 P.2d 1299, 1301 (1975), and an actor is liable for trespass if the actor intentionally enters the land in the possession of another or causes a thing or a third person to do so. Brouch v. State ex rel. Halikowski, 242 Ariz. 611, 620, 399 P.3d 686, 695 (App. 2017); see also Restatement (Second) of Torts § 158 (1965). For an act to be "intentional," it need not be done knowingly—an intentional act occurs when the actor desires the consequences of his act, or believes the consequences are substantially certain to result from it. Id.

As explained more thoroughly herein, the foundation of this dispute is not premised upon the development of your land—it is how the land is being developed, regardless of whether it is in a temporary or permanent state. While you may have a valid building permit that lawfully entitles you to engage in the development of your land, you may not do so to the injury of your neighbors. The intentional change of grading and drainage on your land has caused the presence of a substantial volume of water onto Our Property. We are under no obligation to receive this water and this physical presence entitles us to seek affirmative judicial relief in the form of compensation of damages and injunctive relief. See Champie v. Castle Hot Springs Co., 27 Ariz. 463, (1925) (". . . injunctive relief is a proper remedy against a continued series of trespasses, past and prospective, even when the defendant can respond in money damages . . . .").

Conversely, a cause of action for nuisance is available when a person causes a condition to present an unreasonable interference with another person's use and enjoyment of her property and causes damage. Graber v. City of Peoria, 156 Ariz. 553, 555 (App. 1988). The determination of whether something constitutes an unreasonable interference with use and enjoyment is determined by the injury caused by the condition, not by the conduct of the party creating it. Id.; see also McQuade v. Tucson Tiller Apartments, Ltd., 25 Ariz. App. 312, (1975) (holding that a determination of private nuisance should undertake an examination of the totality of the circumstances).

Therefore, it is not the condition of development on your own real property that forms the basis for our claim for nuisance; rather, it is the fact that your development has caused Our Property to unreasonably receive an increased volume of water as a result of the alteration of the natural drainage conditions in the watercourse. As such, in addition to the remedies provided in the causes of action stated herein, we will seek injunctive relief and abatement of the conditions created on your land constituting the nuisance. See Cannon v. Dunn, 145 Ariz. 115, 117 (App. 1985) ("When some actual and sensible or substantial damage has been sustained, the injured landowner may maintain an action for the abatement of the nuisance.").

As explained herein, the substantial development on your Property provides us with viable claims for (1) damages; (2) a temporary and permanent injunction; and (3) attorneys' fees and costs. Despite securing a basic building permit for the Property, no written authorization for the obstruction or diversion of water from a watercourse has—or could have been—provided by the relevant board of ____ County pursuant to A.R.S. § 48-3613.

We are demanding the immediate removal of any and all obstructions of the watercourse, and a restoration of the natural grading and drainage conditions. Please confirm in writing no later than _____, 20__ at 5:00 p.m. Arizona time that the appropriate and necessary corrective measures have been taken.

Very Truly Yours,

_____

If all else fails, you may need to take legal action. And, it would be wise to contact an attorney to assist you with this claim. While the focus of your action should be trying to get the neighbor into compliance with your requests, you may also need to drive this point home by seeking monetary damages. You will probably want to seek an injunction requiring that the neighbor cease the nuisance behavior or be found in contempt of court, and seek monetary damages to compensate you for the loss of value of your home or other identifiable monetary losses caused by the nuisance.

• Trespass and the Trespassing Titleist Golf Balls

While most people think of trespass as a violation of criminal statutes, there is also a claim for civil trespass, which allows a claimant to sue for injury to their property. In Chapter 4, I describe a rather obnoxious neighbor by the name of Dick, who had a problem keeping his own Titleist golf balls in his own yard. He also caused water that should have been on his property to make its way into the home of Joe and Suzette. Both the act of hitting golf balls onto someone else's yard and causing water to push into the yard of another constitute trespass, which would allow for the filing of a lawsuit against Dick. More on Dick and his poor ball-striking abilities later in this book.

For now, just know that "any unauthorized physical presence on another's property is a trespass." The Arizona cases involving trespass claims indicate a requirement that a physical intrusion or entry upon the land or property belonging to someone else is necessary to a successful trespass claim. That is not enough, however, to establish a viable claim. A claimant must show damages, which are usually measured by the cost of restoring damaged property – like vegetation. In other instances, courts award the difference in property value caused by the property damage as the measure of damages, including the difference in market value of the land before, and after, the trespass.

Pro Tip: Don't trespass and don't hit golf balls into your neighbor's yard.

Also, if you fly a drone over someone's yard, you may be trespassing. So, be mindful of that. And, if a drone is flying over your home, do not take out a gun and blow it up like one neighbor did. This only makes things worse. Send something like this:

SAMPLE

To:_____ Date:_____

Pursuant to Arizona law, you are not authorized to be on the premises known as: [_____]

You are to remove yourself immediately from said premises and not return. You are prohibited from entry onto these premises. Should you be found on the premises at any time from this point forward, you will be removed as authorized by law. This notice is being given to you pursuant to A.R.S. § 13-1501, A.R.S. § 13-1502, A.R.S. § 13-1504 and common law. Should Owner/Agent be required to have you removed, the Owner/Agent reserves the right to request all legal remedies available to him/her including payment of any attorney's fees and court costs which may be incurred.

Hand-delivered: this __day of _____, 20__ . .

By: _____

If you need to file a lawsuit for trespass, just make sure you have legitimate, quantifiable damages. The bent blades of your grass caused by your neighbor's trespass or the soccer ball that landed in your yard probably do not amount to much. But, ruined vegetation and mud tracks from your neighbor's monster truck probably do.

• The Lawful Stealing of Property: Adverse Possession/ Prescriptive Easements/Boundary by Acquiescence

Most folks do not know where their property lines begin and those of their neighbor's end. Often, exact property lines have been lost in the numerous times property has changed hands over the years. Or, people assume their property boundaries are consistent with existing fences or landscape boundaries. This chapter contains information to help you determine exact property lines, where property lines should be, and what you can do if your neighbor starts using your property without permission, either intentionally or unintentionally.

In the following text, the concept of "squatter's rights" are discussed. These rights are usually determined through concepts of adverse possession, prescriptive easements, and boundary by acquiescence. Just ask Roger and Dina.

"Just make sure that fucking troll doesn't block my access routes or put his fence anywhere near my easements" Roger said to me, as I took a swig of coffee. "You see, Patrick, the deputies do not arrive in my neck of the woods for at least 40 minutes, so, we take justice into our own hands out this way if we have to." As Roger said those words, he pulled up his shirt and showed me what he called his "peacemaker." "I see what you mean," I replied, as I wrote down a few more notes.

Roger and his wife Dina had lived in their home for 25 years and enjoyed its expansive, 5 acre setting. They also enjoyed their existing neighbors and how each always "minded their own Goddamn business and helped each other when needed."

Jeff, Roger's new neighbor, owned the vacant 5-acres of land across the street from Roger and Dina. For years, Roger has used portions of Jeff's southern boundary as an access-way to other roads. Roger and Dina's "good" neighbors used the same roadway as well. It was far easier to utilize Jeff's southern boundary to access other roads than to use the road Roger and his neighbors lived on, as that road was bumpier and it did not provide outlets to the roads that led to Roger's job at a plant.

When Jeff arrived on scene, he never introduced himself,

never waved, and worse yet, he tapped into the water system that provided well water to Roger and Dina's home, and about four of their other neighbors. Roger tried to speak with Jeff about tapping into the water system, but Jeff told him to "eat shit" because, according to Jeff, he received a right to tap into the water system by virtue of buying his land. He did not, and Roger knew this. So, Roger cutoff his water supply and thought it was great when water trucks began having to supply water to Jeff's land.

About 6 months after their initial spat, Jeff resurfaced. This time, he began placing piles of debris on the access routes at the southern portion of his property. The piles of debris, which consisted of dead desert vegetation, rocks, and dirt piles, made it impossible for Roger, or anyone else in the neighborhood to use the access route. Again, Roger tried to speak with Jeff and was met with additional un-pleasantries. Roger then reached out to me.

I suggested sending Jeff a certified letter outlining Jeff's inability to cut off the southern access route and further letting him know of the legal basis for the water supply issue that Roger appropriately dealt with earlier in the year. Did I think that Jeff would respond positively to this letter? Nope. Not at all. Based on what he had done, there was no way my letter would talk any sense into Jeff. But, it would put Jeff on notice that Roger and Dina had valid legal claims and that, if Roger and Dina were forced to file a lawsuit, they could point to the letter when asking the Court to require Jeff reimburse them for their legal fees. And, that's exactly what happened.

I wrote Jeff a letter. He received it, and he sent me a love letter in return, which ended with "See Ya In court." And, "Eat Shit." We did see him in court and won an injunction against him requiring him to remove his debris on the southern boundary. We also obtained a judgment, which confirmed that Roger and Dina acquired rights in Jeff's southern boundary by virtue of having a prescriptive easement. Through the judgment, the court also awarded Roger and Dina all of their attorneys' fees.

Jeff, of course, was infuriated, and took the case all the way to the Supreme Court and the Supreme Court declined to change the judgment. Jeff then placed more debris in the access route, and Roger and Dina won more in attorneys' fees. They even had Jeff jailed. Roger and Dina are now planning to own Jeff's property by virtue of enforcing the unpaid monetary portion of their judgment. After losing his land and having his wages garnished by Roger and Dina, the hope of Roger and Dina is that Jeff will not have any money for food and will be forced to eat, well, you know, shit.

The doctrines of prescriptive easements and of adverse possession (which is more widely discussed then prescriptive easements) are bizarre legal concepts, which are now deeply imbedded into our legal system. Under the doctrine of adverse possession, your neighbor may be legally taking your property. Indeed, a person who trespasses onto and possesses the property of another can, after enough time has passed and if certain other conditions are met, become the legal owner of your property. This seeming reward to "squatters" condones trespassing by rewarding trespassers for activities that seem at odds with the concept of property ownership.

You may be asking yourself why these, and the other boundary related doctrines, exist.

Adverse possession actually exists to cure defects in real estate title by putting a timeframe on potential litigation over ownership of property. Because of the doctrine, a landowner can be secure in his title to land. Otherwise, long-lost heirs of any former owner, possessor, or lien holder could come forward with a legal claim on the property. The doctrine of adverse possession prevents this.

In other words, the law rewards a person who possesses the land of another for a requisite period of time, thus encouraging the productive use of land.

Still not understanding why this law exists and how this is a cure? Perhaps the history of the law may help.

One of the earliest recognitions of adverse possession dates back to about 2000 B.C. in the Code of Hammurabi, which explained that if a man left his house, garden, or field and another person possessed and used it for three years, the newcomer retained the land. Ancient Romans believed a person who possessed land nurtured the spirit of the land and gained a greater "ownership" in the land than the title owner.

And, of course, in early England, which is where most of our real estate laws came from, the King generally owned all the land, but when disputes between private individuals began to arise, the actual possession of property was the best evidence of its ownership. At the time, the actual land records were difficult to read and understand, and literacy rates were very low. Thus, showing on proof of possession was, by far, the easiest way of handling ownership disputes.

Through the years, legislatures have created statutes of limitations that specify the length of time that owners have to recover possession of their property from adverse possessors. Although the elements of an adverse possession action are different in every jurisdiction, a person claiming adverse possession is usually required to prove non-permissive use of the property that is actual, open and notorious, exclusive, adverse and continuous for the statutory period. These requirements to prove adverse possession are stringent enough that the doctrine is infrequently applied and is typically granted where a person has actually occupied, cared for, and paid taxes on the property.

In addition to the ability of a neighbor to take your property by virtue of adversely possessing it, your neighbor may be acquiring easement rights in your property. A prescriptive easement is a property interest acquired through a party's unauthorized use of another's real property for a certain period of time. Think trail, or path, or pipes traversing under your property that contain sewage from your neighbor's home. If that party can prove their use met the required elements, which are very similar to the elements of a claim for adverse possession, the party obtains a right to use a specific portion of the property for a specific use by virtue of having a prescriptive easement. Because a prescriptive easement is by definition established without the landowner's consent, and because it can have a significant impact on the property's value and marketability, its appearance can be a most unwelcome surprise. Unlike adverse possession, prescriptive easements typically do not usually require exclusivity. In other words, multiple neighbors, or others, may be acquiring an interest in your land without you knowing it – just like Roger, Dina, and their neighbors did with Jeff's southern boundary.

In addition to adverse possession and the concept of prescriptive easements, there is yet another legal concept meant to clean up boundary issues, which reminds me of Robert Frost's quote, "Good fences make good neighbors." That concept is boundary by acquiescence.

Buying or selling property often uncovers boundary encroachments. Without a way to transfer small slivers of land to the adjoining plot, transferring or deeding the land would be difficult if not impossible. Acquiescence, which is the friendlier sister to adverse possession, is one method of establishing or re-establishing a boundary line different than what may appear.

But, what does boundary by acquiescence actually mean?

Acquiescence means that there are two property owners and a mistake. Both are mistaken about where the real boundary lies. The error about the boundary line is mutual, not the result of hostile action. Three situations apply to acquiescence in most states.

1. There is a dispute, then an agreement.
2. Acquiescence occurs after a statutory period.
3. Acquiescence arises from the intention to deed to a boundary line.

The final situation, i.e., where there was an intent to deed to a specific boundary line, means a property owner intends to deed the property with the boundary line but uses an incorrect description or delineation of the boundary line. Acquiescence to, or approval of, the intended boundary fixes the error.

Much of the law surrounding acquiescence differs from state to state in its particulars. States may create a restriction through a statute of limitations before acquiescence can be applied, or the court may make the final decision of the boundary line regardless of what the landowners say. For example, in Utah, the state supreme court ruled that proof of ownership by both landowners is not required for establishing a boundary line through acquiescence. The court decision was in response to the state's failure to separate acquiescence from agreement. The court held that an owner can acquire property by acquiescence if the owner occupies part (usually a strip) of a neighbor's land "in a visible manner" without objection.

Landowners have one incentive for settling a boundary dispute by acquiescence, at least in some states. Utah imposes property taxes on the encroaching landowner if the boundary is shifted through adverse possession. The tax is not imposed if the boundary moves through acquiescence.

When does acquiescence apply? Boundary issues, as noted

before, often come up during a land sale or when a boundary survey has been performed for some reason. The question of acquiescence comes about when the boundary observed by the landowners for a long time is different from the deed, so it is different than adverse possession. For acquiescence, the mistake is a well-known and an accepted one that has been allowed to stand for an extended period of time. The dispute is always with the adjoining landowner and always about the boundary between the parcels, and it's not really a "dispute" – it's an agreement. In adverse possession, the property can be claimed by anyone. They don't need to be a property owner or on land adjoining the property in dispute, and there must be adversity – i.e., there is no consent to the current status of the boundary lines. Through acquiescence, the boundary is shifted through mutual permission, even if passive.

Pro Tips: Because boundary disputes are unrecorded, i.e., they do not arise due to recorded documents, their presence will not be revealed by the typical due diligence process when purchasing a property. Nor will they necessarily be obvious to you, as a homeowner. There are, however, steps a buyer and property owner can take to lessen the chance of an undisclosed boundary war is taking place.

1. Obtain a Physical Inspection of Property, Aerials, and, Consider Speaking with the Neighbors

Prior to purchasing a property and during its ownership, buyers and existing owners should consider walking the property with a surveyor, reviewing the property lines and locating improvements to look for signs of use by neighbors, and others. For instance, look for trails, paths, tire tracks, and structures not included on the survey. Most prescriptive easements relate to a party passing over and on top of property, like Roger and Dina's situation. They can also arise underneath property, such as when a neighbor uses a drainage line underneath your property, which starts elsewhere.

If your property is particularly large, a review of aerial photographs might be useful. The bird's eye perspective on several web applications (e.g., google) can also help identify uses that are more readily seen from a distance (e.g., a path across property which is well-worn in certain areas and near invisible in others). Additionally, the buyer may interview neighboring landowners and tenants about their use of the property, and whether agreements exist between the seller and neighbor.

2. Title Insurance

Due to the unrecorded nature of many prescriptive easements, a review of your title records will not likely help to identify an issue. You may, however, purchase title insurance, which can allocate the risk of a boundary issue from you to your title insurer.

Under very basic title insurance policies, you likely have no insurance coverage for "unrecorded easements and claims of easements." However, you may be able to purchase an alternative form of title insurance to eliminate this risk, putting the obligation on the title company to accept the risk of a boundary problem.

Additionally, if you provide the title company with an acceptable survey, you may be able to obtain an "endorsement" to your title insurance policy, which provides that the insured land is the same as that shown on the survey. And, if it is later discovered that a prescriptive easement, or adverse possession, existed at the time the policy was issued, and the survey did not include the rights of another in your property, the title company would be responsible to clean up the matter.

3. Consent and Self-Help

If a landowner has identified the party using its property without consent, and if the use has not existed for the statutory period, the most effective manner to thwart the threat of someone taking your property is to provide express and written consent to the user to use your property. By virtue of consenting, the "adverse" element is then lost and no prescriptive easement can be established.

There are various ways you can accomplish this, including providing a revocable and non-transferable license or written agreement – like the one described in Chapter 4. Either one of these options will need to contain the scope and location of the permitted use, state the permitted users, and explain how and when the permission can be revoked.

You may also consider using "self-help" methods to stop someone from taking your property, such as posting "no trespass" signs, erecting fences to interrupt the use, or sending notices demanding that the use stop. However, there is a risk with these methods. If the use continues after the self-help measure, and the owner makes no further efforts to prevent it, the self-help act may then become evidence that the use was in fact adverse. Make sense? If you do not follow up and the use continues, your self-help, while self-serving, will not actually stop the improper use.

When, for example, you own undeveloped land, or you own land in rural areas that are not often monitored, and you are unaware of any specific threat or identifiable user of your property, but you nonetheless believe there is the potential for use and taking of your property, you should still consider issuing a "consent" to unknown users. For instance, signs stating something to the effect of "Private property," "Permission to use that may be revoked at any time" may assist in avoiding an issue. Bottom line – you should determine whether the state in which the property sits has codified language for signs to defeat the adverse element.

• **Neglected Bush: Trim Your Tree, Tim!**

Jen and Ken lived in a North Phoenix home directly next door to Pam and Tim. The neighbors were, by all appearances, friendly with one another. They often waved to one another and exchanged hellos and good mornings. That was until Jen and Ken asked one simple favor: Would you mind trimming your tree?

The tree in question was situated on the south-western portion of Pam and Roger's property and was estimated to be approximately fifty feet in height. While the tree's trunk was located entirely within the boundaries of Pam and Tim's property, the limbs, branches, and outgrowing vegetation extended across the boundary of Jen and Ken's property. And, Jen and Ken, prior to asking that fateful question, found that the tree's roots had begun to encroach across the boundary wall of the property underneath the soil and into Jen and Ken's property.

Jen and Ken did not request the tree trimming because of the way the tree looked as it overhung into their property (even though it was an ugly tree). Rather, the underground roots had damaged pavers and a cement walkway installed on their property. The roots had actually caused the uplifting and cracking of the pavers and walkway. And, more importantly, at least to Ken, the continuous debris, shedding, and sap discharge from the tree always seemed to land on the boat that he stored near the eastern boundary of his yard. Every time Ken went to pull his boat from his backyard, he would have to power wash the boat, dust bust the interior, and then wash the stickiness from his hands and clothing.

When Jen and Ken informed Pam and Tim of their concerns

about the tree, they were met with a smile, and a couple of friendly nods, and an indication that the tree would be addressed in some fashion. As they made their way back to their home, Jen and Ken felt good about the conversation. Later that night, however, they woke up to their dog barking and saw someone running from their front yard. The following morning, Ken walked around his front yard and noticed something strange at the base of the 2 trees in his front yard – several copper stakes were nailed into his trees.

Ken had no clue why there were copper stakes nailed into his trees or what it might mean for their health. So, Ken went to his local hardware store and asked the clerk about large stakes in his trees. The clerk went on to remark that copper stakes are often used to kill large trees without having to cut them down and that, just yesterday, someone had actually asked him how to kill large trees without detection.

After speaking with the clerk, Ken realized what occurred. Pam and Tim were not happy about the request to trim their large tree and sought to surreptitiously get even by killing Jen and Ken's trees. Ken decided not to tell his wife about his discovery and, instead, confronted his neighbors on his own. Of course, Pam and Tim denied knowing anything about the stakes and claimed they would never do such a thing.

Tensions eased a bit for the next 30 or so days, until Ken decided to ask Tim about trimming the tree. As Ken approached Tim's front door, Tim walked from his garage and demanded that Ken get off his lawn and that he get off his property. Ken complied.

Over the next week, Tim decided that he'd turn the otherwise quiet street into a NASCAR racetrack and did multiple burnouts in front of Jen and Ken's home; raced down the street while children were loading onto school buses; and, he played 80s music at the highest volume possible in his garage into the late hours of the night.

Jen and Ken decided to contact the police and got nowhere. According to the police department, this was a "civil matter" and Jen and Ken ought to file a lawsuit to have the tree cut down and, if the noise and obnoxious behavior was so bad, they ought to file an injunction against harassment. They did both.

Jen and Ken filed a lawsuit against Pam and Tim, and, of course, for no reason other than to force the spending of thousands of dollars in court costs and attorneys' fees, Pam and Tim denied liability and forced the case all the way to a trial. And, when a judgment was entered against Pam and Tim, which included an order that they cut down the offending branches of the tree; an order that they take care of the subterranean roots; and an order that they pay all attorneys' fees in favor of Jen and Ken, an appeal was filed by Pam and Tim, which they lost almost immediately.

With an appellate court ruling in hand, which also included an order that they trim their tree and ensure that it no longer encroach onto Jen and Ken's property, and an order that Pam and Roger pay $45,000 in attorneys' fees, Pam and Tim finally gave up. They listed their home for sale and paid Jen and Ken to release the judgment. Not surprisingly, they never disclosed to the new buyer the existence of the problematic tree. Yup, all of this nonsense over a tree.

Trees, bushes, shrubs, and other types of vegetation, and their root systems, often grow above, below, and across boundary lines. And, in some cases, what starts as a small overgrowth can quickly become thousands in attorneys' fees, cars doing burnouts in front of your home, loud music being blasted, and the exchange of a number of un-pleasantries. Believe it or not, the overhanging of trees across and beneath boundary lines and boundary walls actually constitutes trespass, is possibly a legal nuisance, and may constitute negligence if there are damages that result.

Pro Tip: What can you (lawfully) do to stop your neighbor's vegetation? Cut off the offending branch. Yes, that's right. A homeowner can, with or without notice, cut off the branches or roots at the property line. You can also sue for damages and an injunction (i.e., a court order instructing that the vegetation be removed), so long as some "actual and sensible or substantial damage" occurs. Oh, and be careful to not destroy or kill your neighbor's vegetation if you decide to cut off the offending branches.

CHAPTER THREE

Agreements Among Neighbors

"If you burn your neighbor's house down, it doesn't make your house look any better."

— *Lou Holtz*

• John and His Easements

John owned a parcel of land near Tucson and had the right to use two separate access easements over property owned by others – (1) a driveway easement over the property to his east, owned by Milton; and (2) a secondary access easement over a separate parcel (also owned by Milton). The secondary access easement granted John the limited right to use a strip of land as a "secondary right of way" for "emergency ingress and egress, only."

Instead of utilizing the driveway easement as the primary method to access his property, John utilized the secondary access easement for primary driveway purposes because, according to John, it was smoother and had better grading. Once he realized what was going on, Milton installed wood dividers and a heavy chain link fence, thereby impeding and slowing down John's access to his home via the secondary access easement, which made accessing John's property much less convenient.

John then filed suit against Milton arguing that Milton was trespassing on John's easement and creating a nuisance. During the litigation, John acknowledged that he, and members of his family, used the secondary access easement on a daily basis and argued that he should not be stuck having to deal with opening a fence or gate when using "his" easement.

The court threw out John's case. And, no, I did not represent John. I, fortunately, represented Milton. Why was it thrown out? Here, the secondary access easement was so limited in scope that it did not allow for other uses. Indeed, it was to be utilized for secondary and emergency access, only. John, therefore, was not entitled to expand its use by utilizing it for primary access purposes. The Court did note, however, that John's use of the secondary access easement for 10 years could have resulted in a lawful expansion if John could establish the elements of a prescriptive easement.

John's case was an important reminder to Milton and to anyone else who notices that an easement is being misused. Do not allow the party using an easement on your land to exceed the scope of your easement. You, Milton, and other property owners should monitor the use of easements for any use that may be unauthorized – whether the use is of a driveway, access to mailboxes, or other accommodations.

An easement is a right that one party has to use the property of another for a specific purpose. The property benefitting from an easement is called the "dominant estate" and the property burdened by an easement is called the "servient estate." Sounds straightforward, would you agree? And, the word "easement" even has the word "ease" in it, so, these cannot be too difficult to understand, right? Far from it.

There are numerous types of easements that may currently

affect your property and that you may need to consider granting, or even selling, to others. For example, there are easements for grazing, utilities, avigation, HOAs, railroads, streets, drainage, driveways, recreation, and, of course, access. There are also "view" easements that prohibit the construction of improvements on a property so that homeowners can enjoy certain views. And, there are mutual easements, cross-easements, and temporary easements.

There are also "implied" easements, which usually arise when a property owner divides property into smaller parts and one part of the land derives benefit from another party. Basically, an implied easement is the result of a legal presumption that, whenever a party conveys property to another, he is conveying whatever is necessary for the beneficial use of the conveyed property.

Confused (or bored) yet? There's more. Whenever a landlocked property owner needs to become "unlocked," the landlocked property owner, who may be a neighbor of yours, may be entitled to a private way of necessity over your property, and the process to obtain this type of easement is similar to a condemnation action. In other words, one of your neighbors may be able to condemn your property and obtain an easement over your property.

Pro Tips: If you want to draft an easement with a neighbor, consider the following tips. Again, easements can be complicated, but the following are common to almost all easements:

First, determine the type of easement to be granted. If the easement you are granting will benefit land, you will be granting an "easement appurtenant." And, in this type of situation, you must specifically identify the burdened and benefitted properties. In other words, you need to reference two separate properties in your easement agreement – the land that will benefit from the easement being granted and the land that will host, or be burdened by, the easement. Contrarily, if the easement you are granting is intended to benefit a person, it is considered an "easement in gross" and you, therefore, must properly identify the person being provided with the rights.

Second, identify the parties to the easement. The person providing the easement, i.e., you or your neighbor, is the "grantor." The person receiving the easement is the grantee. And, unless you are limiting the duration of the easement, once your document is recorded, the easement will "run with the land" and will burden (or benefit) all of the subsequent owners of your land and those of your neighbor.

Third, indicate the nature of the easement. Be specific. Providing an easement for "access," which may mean vehicular to your neighbor, but only pedestrian access to you, could spell trouble. Similarly, even if the parties intended for vehicular access, you could be stuck with large trucks or other unintended vehicles using the easement, like ATVs or semi-trucks, if you do not further define what constitutes a vehicle.

Fourth, identify any rights that you want to continue to have in the easement area. For instance, if you want to place a gate at the point of access, specifically include that right in your agreement.

Fifth, if the easement is not perpetual, i.e., if it is temporary in nature, be sure to specify the date, or event, upon which the easement will terminate.

Sixth, address various miscellaneous issues. For example, who is responsible for maintaining and restoring the easement? What about taxes? What about indemnification and insurance obligations if someone is injured while using the easement? How about a payment for the purchase and sale of the easement? Most easements are valuable and you may need to obtain an appraiser to value the easement. Will your easement be exclusive or non-exclusive? In other words, can you grant a similar easement over the same space to someone else?

And, finally, notarized signatures and depictions of the easements should be recorded with the County Recorder. Otherwise, third parties will have no idea about the easement or the rights conveyed via the agreement you drafted.

If you want to terminate an easement, or believe one should be (or has been) terminated, here are a few things to watch out for:

Expiration – look at the language in the agreement itself to determine whether, by its express terms, the easement no longer exists.

Release – look to determine whether there is a writing signed by both the grantor and the grantee, or subsequent owners, that terminates the easement. Both parties to an easement agreement must sign a release to terminate an easement.

Merger – sometimes an owner of the easement acquires title to both the benefitted and burdened estates. In such a case, the easement may be gone by virtue of a merger of these two estates.

Abandonment – If your neighbor acts as if the easement no longer exists, e.g., the neighbor is no longer maintaining the roadway and using an alternative route, your neighbor may have abandoned the easement.

• Real Estate Licenses

And, no, we're not talking about real estate licenses allowing one to assist clients to buy or sell homes. We're talking about a license to use something, or do something, on a neighbor's property. Licenses to use the land of another are not typically the subject of litigation. So, I've got no anecdotes or stories for you. Nevertheless, licenses to use someone else's property are important agreements for neighbors and the pro tips are worth considering.

A license is not an easement. A license is usually not permanent. So, irrespective of whether or not there is permission and continuous use of someone else's property, the land or area being used cannot turn into an easement (or a prescriptive easement). A license just provides a party with the privilege of using your land for a certain purpose for a set duration. For instance, say you want to provide your neighbor with the right to cross through your backyard to get to a hiking trail or bike path. In this situation, you can provide your neighbor with a license to access your property and can revoke the license to use your backyard at any time, in which case your neighbor would be trespassing if your neighbor continues to use your backyard. You have the power to condition the use of your backyard and the time constraints for its use. Compare this to an easement, which can only be terminated if both the property owners subject to the easement agree to terminate it.

Pro Tips: Make sure you are providing a license if that is what you are willing to provide to your neighbor. In other words, don't accidentally grant an easement. Easements and licenses can look similar and often contain similar language. If a court has to decide whether you provided an easement or a license, you're in trouble.

Consider charging no fee, or a very nominal one, for the license. Easements are typically more valuable than a license because of their permanence. So, landowners sell easements, whereas, with a license, landowners give away something fairly insignificant because it can be revoked at any time.

Put your license in writing. I've seen licenses for the use of pools, the use of backyards for kids to play baseball, and, I've seen a trampoline license (i.e., one neighbor granted access to his backyard for others to play on his trampoline).

Warning: there are several instances in which a license can

actually be converted into something more permanent – i.e., an easement. If, with your knowledge, the person benefitting from the license improves the space licensed to them by, for example, putting pavers on the walkway, grading the trail, or the like, the license could be converted to an easement.

• Wrong, Ron: The Deed Restriction that Took Down a House

It was a long drawn out court battle. There was a trial, followed by an appeal, followed by a request that the Supreme Court overturn the lower court's decision. It wasn't happening. Ron's request for one last review of his situation and his obvious efforts to delay the inevitable were done.

Carolyn, Ron's neighbor of 12 years and his adversary for the last 5 years, sat back secretly wishing things could be different. At the private entrance down the hill from both of their large, custom homes entered an officer from the sheriff's department, a bulldozer, an excavator, and a crew of about 10 contractors. The day had finally come to knock down the $1million second story addition to Ron's home.

Ron, a successful real estate agent, purchased his home in the mid-2000s and made his mark in the real estate world during the real estate boom going on at the same time. He purchased a home in Camelback Estates, which was one the most exclusive addresses in town. It is tough to describe the orientation of Ron's home to Carolyn's home, as no one in this area had a real "next door" neighbor. It wasn't easy to even get to the home "next" to Carolyn's as it required an uphill walk of a few hundred yards – hardly "next door" in the traditional sense. At the time Ron purchased his home, prices for similar homes in the neighborhood were in the $700-$800 per square foot range.

The homes in this private, gated community were at the base of

Camelback Mountain. There were 12 homes in the neighborhood and it took about 5 minutes on a winding road to arrive at Ron's home (and Carolyn's, as well). The views from these homes were spectacular. Ron and Carolyn were both up a 10th of the way on the mountain itself and had views of the city, various parks, golf courses, and, the twinkling city lights at night. Because of these views, the original owners of these homes recorded a deed restriction to preserve the feel of the neighborhood and the expansive views.

In connection with purchasing the home, Ron received a package of title documents from the title company, but he never bothered to review the documents. Or rather, he reviewed the documents and did not believe they applied to him, as he later confirmed during a deposition. He just wanted to enhance his views and had a budget of $1million to do it.

Five years ago, when contractors began appearing at Ron's home, Carolyn began to get anxious. She had never discussed anything of real substance with Ron and barely saw him. On a hot morning in May, Carolyn returned from a walk and noticed more traffic than usual and that trusses had been installed on Ron's roof. She flagged down one of the roofers who was taking a cigarette break and asked him what was going on. "An addition" he replied. A what? What type of addition? "A big one, with a winding staircase, a loft, and an observation deck. Do you want to see the plans?" Of course she wanted to see them.

When Carolyn initially viewed the plans, she remarked at how beautiful the addition appeared on paper. Secretly, however, she was boiling. Ron's addition would partially obscure her views of portions of the mountain. She wondered how Ron could do something like this without ever consulting his neighbors.

As Carolyn later discovered, Ron could not do any of this

without a complete amendment to the deed restrictions – the deed restrictions that Ron never bothered to read or appreciate. Had he actually paid attention to the restrictions, he would have noticed what Carolyn knew, which is that the homes in this neighborhood could be single story homes, and only single story homes. In fact, although a bit archaic, Paragraph 4 of the deed restrictions was pretty clear: "[n]o structure shall be erected, altered, placed or permitted to remain on any of the lots other than one single-story detached single-family dwelling and a private garage, and a guest or servant quarters."

After multiple attempts to discuss his project and no response from Ron, Carolyn requested injunctive relief, i.e., a court order halting construction until the Court had a full opportunity to review the matter. She received her injunction and construction stopped for weeks.

Ron's argument, which works every once in a while, was that circumstances in the neighborhood, and everywhere else for that matter, had changed such that the deed restrictions no longer made sense. Under the doctrine of changed circumstances, a court may render a deed restriction unenforceable if there has been a fundamental change in circumstances which would defeat or frustrate the original purpose of the restriction. In short, "the doctrine of changed circumstances" may relieve a party against the enforcement of a deed restriction if conditions have so changed since the making of the restrictions.

Basically, Ron's argument was that the deed restrictions were so old and no longer made sense because, according to the argument: "people should be able to use their homes the way they want to" and "society prefers homes that are worth more and have more square footage, because they are the most profitable."

Wrong, Ron, the trial court judge ruled. And, with that, Ron's million-dollar project and the Court's ruling were on their way to the Court of Appeals for further review.

The other argument asserted by Ron was that Carolyn, and half of the other owners in the neighborhood were, themselves, in violation of one or more of the other requirements contained in the deed restrictions. Again, Ron, wrong. Ron could separately seek to enforce the restrictions against the violating owners, but he could not use this as a defense to stop his addition from being bulldozed, and bulldozed it was.

Deed restrictions, sometimes referred to as restrictive covenants, or in Ron and Carolyn's case, the "Declaration of Restrictive Covenants of Camelback Estates" are contained in a deed, or in a separately recorded document. These restrictions usually "run with the land" meaning that anyone who ever buys a property with restrictions is supposed to honor them. This may include situations like Ron, where the restrictions are more than 50 years old, and/or were put in place when the neighborhood looked much different.

Deed restrictions can cover almost anything, including: the number of bedrooms; number of vehicles in the driveway; paint colors; whether or not animals are permitted; the ability to operate a business in the home; the architectural type of the home (e.g., Spanish, colonial, modern, etc.); and whether or not pools, sheds, gazebos, and pergolas are allowed in backyards.

Just about the only things contained in deed restrictions that cannot be enforced are covenants relating to racial or religious limitations. Oftentimes in the early part of the 20th century, developers and homeowners included restrictions on who could purchase and own certain homes. These restrictions are, of course, no longer valid.

Pro Tips: Deed restrictions turn up during a title search of property. So, prior to purchasing a property, take a look at your title commitment and the underlying title documents provided to you. And, of course, review the documents prior to any major additions or renovations to confirm that they are allowed. Don't be like Ron and have to beg for forgiveness from his neighbors or the court.

Just assuming that deed restrictions are inapplicable or too old to be enforced is a bad idea, but homeowners do it all the time. Oftentimes, homeowners like Ron also think that only an HOA or governing body can enforce deed restrictions, and if there is no HOA or governing body, the restrictions cannot be enforced. Wrong again, Ron. Most courts allow individual homeowners to enforce deed restrictions without the need for a governing board, just like Carolyn did.

What if I do not like the deed restriction and want it changed? Good luck. Modifying a deed restriction can be tough. First, look for an expiration date in the document. If the restrictions have expired, you should be good to go. Second, some documents allow for waivers or ways to deviate from strict requirements of a restriction. And, if all else fails, you may be able to invalidate a deed restriction by seeking a judicial declaration that the restriction is too vague to understand, it has expired, it is illegal, or, it is, and has been, disregarded by neighbors and is therefore abandoned.

• Farmer Joe's Agreement to Share His Water Lines

Dehydrated horses, unbathed clients, and dead plants are oftentimes the direct result of a poorly drafted, or misinterpreted, well share agreement. In rural areas, well share agreements are actually quite common.

Take a look at what happened to Bert, the purchaser of a large horse property subject to a well share agreement. Bert purchased a

property from Dave, who represented, and truly believed, that the well subject to the well share agreement affecting Dave's property was sufficient to provide water to occupants of Dave's home and to the irrigation system for Dave's property, which supplied water to numerous plants around his house. In reality, the well serving the irrigation system was on a farmer's adjacent property and could only be used with his permission.

About a year after purchasing Dave's home, Bert, by mistake, allowed his horses to use portions of the farmer's land as their restroom. Infuriated by this "disrespect," the farmer cut off the irrigation water usage. When Bert realized that his water had been shut off and that he had been trespassing on the farmer's property, Bert apologized to the farmer and the farmer re-engaged the irrigation water usage with conditions. It was then discovered that all of the confusion stemmed from the original parties' failure to sufficiently identify the well in the original well share agreement.

There are relatively few cases dealing with well share agreements, but, the cases that do address well sharing agreements are largely centered around the interpretation of certain provisions contained in the agreements themselves. This is because a well share agreement is just a contract relating to the drilling, maintaining, and use of a well.

Pro Tips: As a contract, a well share agreement must address certain key provisions, including the identity of the parties, the property, the well and distribution system, easements, maintenance requirements, and the remedies for failing to honor the obligations contained in the contract.

Additionally, it is wise to properly identify, with legal descriptions and depictions, the location of the well and its distribution system.

Identifying the purpose for having a well share agreement is similarly of critical importance. The parties to the document should indicate whether the use of the water will be seasonal, periodic, or continuous and whether the water is to be used for domestic, agricultural, or commercial purposes.

Once parties, properties, and the purpose of the well share agreement have been articulated, the agreement should address the party responsible for the installation, operation, and maintenance of the well, and the costs associated with each of these items. Requiring the installation of individual water and electric meters for each water connection is helpful for avoiding future claims of over usage or underpayments. It is also helpful to identify the party responsible for contacting third parties to maintain or fix well related issues.

In a well share agreement, parties must usually grant mutual non-exclusive easements to one another for accessing the well house and the water distribution systems for various reasons. Hire a surveyor for this.

A well drafted well share agreement includes a section about conveying one of the properties to a buyer. In fact, most agreements should include a reference to what happens when a property subject to a well share agreement is conveyed to another party.

Remember Roger and Dina's scenario outlined above? In Roger and Dina's scenario outlined in the prescriptive easement chapter, the issue of whether the well share agreement and water rights well conveyed to subsequent purchasers (in addition to the prescriptive easement problem) was an issue for the parties. There were no water rights conveyed to Jeff, despite his insistence that he received these rights. Indeed, the court ultimately found Jeff had no right to use the water system Roger and Dina owned because there was no reference in the document to subsequent purchasers.

Other important terms to include are those pertaining to enforcing the agreement (like, what happens if there is a dispute over payments or usage – do we find a mediator to resolve the dispute, cut off everyone's water until an agreement is reached, etc.) and what to do if someone is not paying their fair share.

Note: Some lenders require specific language in order to finance properties subject to well share agreements. Parties should draft the well share agreement and any amendments to conform to their lenders' requirements as well as applicable federal, state, and local laws.

Here is a sample of a well share agreement:

WELL SHARE AGREEMENT

1. RECITALS.

On or about _____, _____purchased two adjacent five (5) acre lots of land in _____, Arizona. On or about _____, _____ subdivided the southern lot into two equal lots of two and one half acres each. _____ retained ownership of Parcel _____ and sold Parcel _____ on or about _____ to _____. On _____20__, _____ completed construction on an approved well, Arizona Department of Water Resources Well Registry _____ (hereinafter, the **"Well"**), located on the _____ parcel of land. On or about _____, _____entered a Public Utility and Ingress/Egress Easement in favor of _____ to utilize the Well.

Based upon the foregoing recitals, _____, _____, and _____ (Collectively, the **"Owners"**) hereby agree to the following provisions.

2. EFFECTIVE DATE.

Effective as of the __ day of December, 20__, the Owners enter into this Well Share Agreement ("Agreement").

3. PARTIES, PARCELS, & WELL SHARES.

The Owners agree that ownership of the Well shall be divided into four shares as follows:

Two (2) shares (50%) of the Well use belongs to the Owner of the following parcel:

_____.

One (1) share (25%) of the Well use belongs to the Owner of the following parcel:

_____.

One (1) share (25%) of the Well use belongs to the Owner of the following parcel:

_____.

4. SERVIENT & DOMINANT PARCELS.

a. Servient Parcel. The parcel containing the Easement: Grantor's property located at Maricopa County Parcel _____, which contains the Well.

b. Dominant Parcels. The parcels benefited by the Easements:

Grantee's property located at Maricopa County Parcels _____ and _____.

5. EASEMENTS. For good and valuable consideration, the Owner of the Servient Parcel hereby grant to the Grantee, as Owners of the Dominant Parcels, the following easements:

a. Wellsite Easement. An easement in and across the Servient Parcel (the "Wellsite Easement") for use of the Well located thereon, and the related pump, well head, well house and other equipment and facilities located thereon.

b. Access Easement. An easement for reasonable access to the Well, (an "Access Easement"), in and across the Servient Parcel.

c. Utilities Easement. An easement for underground utilities for the operation of the Well and individual delivery lines, (a "Utilities Easement"), in and across the Wellsite and Access Easements.

6. MAINTENANCE, OPERATION AND EXPENSE.
a. Well.

i. Well Components. The structural, mechanical, and related components of the Well (meaning the improvements and equipment involved in the shared water system and equipment at the wellsite, including but not limited to the submersible pump and motor, valves, control system, electrical equipment, power supply, storage tank, pressure tank, booster pump, etc., and other appurtenances necessary to the production and delivery of water from the Well and storage of water produced by the Well), the well house, (meaning both the structure and any required screening or landscaping), and the water lines shall be deemed "Capital Improvements."

ii. Maintenance, Repair and Reconstruction. As of the effective date of this Agreement, each Owner of the Well shall share equally by their shares of ownership any and all costs of adequate and reasonable maintenance, repair, renewal, replacement and upgrading of the Capital Improvements at the Well, as necessary or appropriate to keep same in a good, safe, neat and clean condition. All other costs associated with redrilling or replacing the Well, together with any and all real estate taxes imposed on the Well and its Capital Improvements, and the costs of any insurance deemed necessary by a majority of the Owners, (collectively, the "Maintenance Expenses"). Each Owner who is hooked up to the Well shall include a reasonable sum, as prescribed by the Well Manager, described below, to build up a reserve of capital for the larger expenditures involved in the maintenance, repair and replacement of the Capital Improvements (the "Reserve for Replacement"). Any Maintenance Expenses or similar capital expenditures, which cannot be covered from such reserves shall be allocated to each

Well Owner, commensurate with their shares of ownership in the Well, as they are incurred and invoiced as they become due, for payment not more than 30 days thereafter. **b. Individual Delivery and Utility Lines.** Each Owner agrees to construct and maintain at its own expense its own individual delivery lines from the Well to a point of use within the boundaries of their parcel, entirely underground, and including metering devices of the same manufacturer as are in use at the Well. The responsibility for maintenance and repair of the individual delivery lines, and underground utilities in association therewith, shall rest with the Owner of the parcel in which the individual delivery line is located.

c. Operation.

i. Operating Costs for Water Use. The "Operating Costs" of the Well shall include, but not be limited to, electrical service to the well pump, and water quality testing, and the responsibility for such payment shall be separate from the Maintenance Expenses described above.

ii. Well Manager. The Maintenance Expenses and Operating Costs shall be collected and accounted for by the "Well Manager", and, at the request of any Owner, and, in the event of any default or uncertainty, shall be the party in whose name the account for the electrical meter on the wellhead is maintained. The initial Well Manager shall be _____.

iii. Operating Account. The sum of $20.00 per month, in sums equal to Well share ownership detailed in Section 3 above, shall be contributed by the Owners to a separate checking account operated by the Well Manager (the "Operating Account") to cover the Maintenance Expenses and Operating Costs and hold the Reserve for Replacement. Each Owner shall be entitled at all times to receive a copy of a current statement of that Operating Account upon request.

iv. Allocation and Payment. Both the electrical meter on the wellhead and the individual water meters on the outgoing lines shall be read on or about the first day of each month by the Well Manager, or someone at his/her discretion who shall then prepare and send invoices for payment not more than 30 days later by each Owner of his pro-rata share of the Operating Costs as determined by the reading on the wellhead meter divided into the monthly meter reading on the individual water meter for each Owner, along with any additional amounts necessary to fund the Reserve for Replacement. Each Owner herewith grants the other Owners, their heirs or assigns, a perpetual right and license to access all meters for purposes of collecting consumption data.

d. Termination of Financial Obligations. Any Owner who wishes to permanently relinquish its rights to use and share in the Well under this Agreement, may do so upon recordation of a notice thereof, and, upon delivery of a copy of the notice as recorded to all other Owners, such withdrawing Owner shall be relieved of all financial obligations under this Agreement which arise thereafter.

7. OTHER CONDITIONS AND LIMITATIONS. The Rights described herein, and the continued enjoyment thereof, are further subject to the following conditions and limitations:

a. Use Within Lot. The Owner of each respective property shall have the right to take water from the Well for their reasonable use on each respective property only. No Owner shall provide water to any other owner on or off the subject property, nor cause to be divided in any manner or assign the rights of this Agreement without the express written consent of all other Owners.

b. Domestic Use. The Owners agree, that no water from the Well shall be used for commercial purposes, but only for their private domestic use including vegetable gardens and livestock maintenance. Domestic use may include maintenance of ponds or swimming pools, which are constructed with an impervious liner to prevent leakage.

8. REPRESENTATIONS & WARRANTIES. The Owners of each parcel hereto mutually acknowledge and understand that: (i.) the present Well characteristics, i.e., well depth and construction, static water level, draw down, yield, and operating capabilities are either known or acceptable to each Owner; (ii.) no warranty is being given by any Owner that there will be at any time water of a quantity or quality produced by the Well for the needs or demands of any Owner; and (iii.) the chemical quality of water from the well has not been measured, but is expected to meet all mandatory Federal, State and local standards for potable water; but (iv.) there is no express or implied warranty made by any Owner hereto that water from the Well shall be of a quality fit for human consumption and/or domestic use.

9. GENERAL PROVISIONS.
a. Multiple Owners. As used in this Agreement: "Owners" shall include all parties who are owners of all or a portion of the parcels described under Section 3 above.
b. Duration and Binding Effect. The covenants, conditions, restrictions and other provisions of this Agreement (the "Restrictions") are for the exclusive benefit and protection of the Owners of the named parcels in Section 3 above, and shall exist in perpetuity and run with the land and be binding upon

all persons who own, lease, sublease, or occupy any property or portion thereof on the date of recordation of this Agreement or thereafter and inure to the benefit of, the present and future owners of all properties, whether or not such is subdivided, and their heirs, devisees, personal representatives, shareholders, directors, officers, employees, receivers, assigns or the like.

c. Waiver or Abandonment. The failure to enforce any breach or violation of any of the Agreement shall not constitute an abandonment or a waiver of any right to enforce such Agreement. **d. Injunctive Relief.** In addition to the remedies for a monetary default provided above, every act or omission whereby any one or more of the provisions herein set forth is violated in whole or in part, where such violation continues for a period of 60 or more days from the date of written notice thereof from the respective Owner, is hereby declared to be a nuisance and may be enjoined or abated, whether or not the relief sought is for negative or affirmative action, and in the event of any violation or threatened violation of any one or more of the provisions herein set forth, the affected Owner may enforce this Agreement by seeking injunctive relief, or monetary damages, but nothing contained herein shall be construed as meaning that damages are an adequate remedy where equitable relief is sought.

e. Disputes. Any dispute arising hereunder shall be construed under Arizona law, with Maricopa County as the choice of venue, and the prevailing party shall also be entitled, as and for a liquidated value of its incidental and consequential damages, to an amount equal to twice its reasonable attorneys' fees and court costs.

f. Severability: Any determination by any court of competent jurisdiction that any provision in this Agreement is invalid or unenforceable shall not affect the validity or enforceability of the remaining provisions of this Agreement and the same shall remain in full force and effect.

g. Entire Agreement. This Agreement, including any related documents referred to herein and attached hereto, constitute the complete understanding and agreement between the Parties. All prior conversations, negotiations and representations of the Parties concerning this Agreement are superseded and merged herein.

h. Amendment. This Agreement may be amended from time to time by recording in the Office of the County Recorder of Maricopa County, Arizona, an instrument in writing reciting said amendment and signed (with signatures properly acknowledged) by the all Owners.

i. Execution: This Agreement may be executed in counterpart, and when fully executed by all parties hereto, and shall become effective when recorded or returned fully executed to all the parties.

IN WITNESS WHEREOF, the undersigned Owners of the parcels hereby accept, approve and execute this Agreement.

GRANTOR:

_____

GRANTEE:

_____

CHAPTER FOUR

Statutes Relating To Neighbor Disputes

"I am a reflection of my community."

— Tupac Shakur, HOA expert
(errr, wait a minute, he was a rap artist)

• "Lien" on Me

Christie owned a modest home in Central Phoenix and ever since her husband left her several years ago, the home had fallen into disrepair. The exterior of the home needed painting, she had some windows that needed to be replaced, and there were a number of overgrown plants and trees in her front and back yards. Her neighbor to the west, Darren, a handyman of some 20 or so years, had recently been divorced himself and found Christie very attractive. He often asked her over to his house for wine, breakfast, movie night, and the like, and was turned down almost every time.

One day, as part of his brilliant plan to win Christie's affection, Darren offered to repaint her home, fix the windows, and remove all of the dead and overgrown vegetation that Christie never seemed to have time to handle. Darren let Christie know that he just wanted to help her out. Christie never really approved of Darren doing the work, but she didn't stop him when he did.

Darren did a fantastic job with Christie's home. It almost looked brand new after all he did for her.

After Darren completed the work, Christie asked if she owed Darren anything for his work. Darren replied, "No, all I ask is that you go to my family holiday party and show me some affection." Christie, completely disgusted by this advance, politely said, no, and that she was not attracted to Darren. She then went back home and did not hear from, or see, Darren for several weeks, which was just fine with her.

She did, however, receive a strange letter about a month later from U.S. Bank, who was the holder of her mortgage loan. In the letter from U.S. Bank there was a reference to a "lien" that had been recorded against her home – i.e., U.S. Bank became aware of a lien recorded against Christie's house and that the lien needed to be paid or released within 30 days or U.S. Bank would take further action. Christie had no clue about any lien, so she quickly contacted her friend who owned a title company. Her friend pulled a title report for Christie's home and found the lien referenced in the letter. Apparently, Darren recorded a lien against Christie's home for the work he completed for her. Correct – he recorded a lien for the work Christie never requested and that Darren did as a way of winning her over.

Liens, judgments, and other improper documents are recorded against title to real estate all of the time. Christie found this out the hard way, as she had to seek immediate court intervention to have the improper lien released.

There are several ways provided by law to remove liens that are recorded against real estate. Whether a lien was filed in error, is a matter of a dispute, or simply was not withdrawn or released when paid, you have options to clear your title when clearing title cannot be accomplished cooperatively. This usually requires you to file a quiet title action or a "special action" under statute.

A hallmark of our legal system is the protection of real estate rights, including the right to have title to your home "clean" from fake, false, or groundless liens. And, in Arizona, it is unlawful to record a groundless document or lien against a real property. Indeed, a person who causes a wrongful document or lien to be recorded against title to your home may be liable for statutory damages of $5,000, or treble the actual damages, whichever is greater, plus reasonable attorney's fees and costs. In addition, a person who records a wrongful document or lien may be guilty of a class 1 misdemeanor.

Examples of documents that may have been improperly recorded against your home include: (1) a mortgage or deed of trust; (2) quit claim deed; (3) conveyance deeds such as general warranty deeds or special warranty deeds; (4) judgments; (5) lis pendens; (6) materialmen's lien; and (7) mechanic's lien.

The legal term for recording false documents is slander of title. Once you can show that the person knew or should have known that the document recorded against title to your home was groundless, the person is liable for damages of $5,000 or more plus attorneys' fees, even if the person later releases the recorded document.

Damages can be quite high in some circumstances. Take, for example, the neighborly situation described above. What if Christie discovered the lien while attempting to sell her property, and the sale failed because the wrongful lien was not released on time? Say, for instance, despite Christie's best efforts to have the lien released prior to the sale, the buyer cancelled the real estate contract and Christie forfeited the earnest money. Once the lien had finally been judicially cleared, Christie sold the property to another buyer but for $40,000 less than the original contract. In this situation, which happens quite often, the handyman was liable to Christie for treble damages of $120,000 (actual damages of $40,000 x 3) plus attorneys' fees.

Note: Darren would have been liable for damages and attorneys' fees without prior written notice and even if the lien was released prior to Christie filing her lawsuit to clear title. Courts have held that neither notice nor a grace period is required to establish liability concerning a wrongful recording. The key is that Darren may be liable for damages of at least $5,000, plus attorneys' fees, regardless of whether the property owner actually suffered any harm from the recording. And if the owner sustained damages, such as a lost sale or missed refinance opportunity, the damages could be much, much higher.

Pro Tip: In addition to the liability described above, false lien statutes provide yet another sanction for those who fail to comply when a written demand is actually provided. The person recording a wrongful document will be liable for $1,000 or treble actual damages, plus attorney fees and costs, if he or she fails to comply with the demand letter within twenty days. These penalties can often be enough to convince someone to either release the lien or negotiate a settlement. Depending on the situation, a properly worded demand letter (there are statutory references that must be made in the letter) may be all that is needed to get a lienholder to release his interest in your title. If a formal demand does not resolve the matter, then the statutes provide a roadmap for pursuing necessary litigation.

Here is a letter to consider using if someone has recorded an improper lien or other recorded document against title to your property:

SAMPLE

Re: Demand for Lien Release Pursuant to A.R.S. § 33-420

Dear _____:

I am the owner of [insert property address/description] (the "Property"). The Property is currently in escrow with a scheduled closing date of ____, 20__. During the course of escrow, the title company recently informed me that a Deed of Trust recorded by _____ , remains as a lien against the Property.

This information came as a complete surprise to me, as I paid the corresponding promissory note in full in 20__. Apparently, however, _____failed to record an appropriate release of the Deed of Trust, which continues to encumber the Property and threatens to jeopardize the transaction.

Please consider this letter a demand that _____ immediately record an appropriate release of the Deed of Trust. Should you fail to do so on or before _____, I intend to file suit against _____ for the violation of A.R.S. § 33-420. This statute provides for the recovery of $5,000.00 or treble actual damages, whichever is greater, against a person or entity responsible for a groundless or otherwise invalid lien. Beyond actual damages, which will include profits from the instant transaction, I will also be entitled to the recovery of attorneys' fees and costs of suit.

We appreciate your prompt attention to this matter and anticipate the immediate removal of this encumbrance.

Sincerely,

_____

Christie also had another claim against Darren for statutory "quiet title." A.R.S § 12-1101 authorizes a quiet title action by anyone having an interest in real property against anyone "claiming" an adverse interest in the same real estate. A quiet title action is typically brought to clear the title – i.e., to "quiet" any dispute over title to property. A quiet title action results in a judgment barring the named defendant, i.e., Darren, or any other lienholder, from ever again asserting or continuing to enforce the adverse interest. In other words, because Darren was making a claim to Christie's property – he made a claim that he has a lien interest in her home – Christie could have filed a quiet title action to judicially rid him of any interest he claimed.

Pro Tip: A homeowner affected by someone's improper claim to title to real estate can, potentially, avoid having to file a lawsuit by sending a demand letter to the person making the improper claim. The letter must request that the person disclaim their alleged interest in the title, and the letter must provide twenty days for the person to comply. If a person fails to comply with the letter, then they will not be entitled to costs if they later disclaim their interest. The letter also triggers the possibility for the harmed homeowner, i.e., Christie, to recover attorneys' fees.

Here is an example of a letter to use. The terms of the letter, and the requests made in the letter, are rather awkward because they must contain certain buzzwords and they must track language outlined in the statute:

SAMPLE

VIA FIRST CLASS MAIL AND CERTIFIED MAIL, RETURN RECEIPT REQUESTED

_____

_____

Re: Demand Pursuant to A.R.S. 12-1103

Dear _____ :

We own real property known as _____ (A.P.N. _____), _____(A.P.N. _____), and _____ (A.P.N. ____). The above properties are depicted on the map attached hereto as Exhibit A, highlighted in green. We write in regards to two specific access route issues in the area of your property, which are also depicted on the attached map and are highlighted in yellow. Your property (A.P.N. _____) is located between _____ and _____Avenue adjacent to our property and is also set forth on the attached map, highlighted in orange. You are receiving this letter because you are the record owner of the property containing the access routes depicted in the attached map.

We have been utilizing the access routes depicted in yellow for more than 20 years. We have done so for ingress and egress to our properties. A prescriptive easement arises after ten years of open and obvious use. A prescriptive easement gives an adjacent landowner the legal right to continue to use an access route when such access route has been used for more than ten years. A prescriptive easement does not change ownership of any property or affect who pays the property taxes. In this case, we have acquired a prescriptive easement over the access routes depicted in the attached map in yellow.

Enclosed is $5.00 cash and a quit claim deed for you to execute and return to me to confirm the right to an access easement in my favor based on the doctrine of prescriptive easement. The $5.00 is submitted to you as required by statute to cover the costs, if any, to have the enclosed quit claim deed notarized. We do not want a fight amongst neighbors, but we do need to obtain a signed document that can be recorded to confirm our access rights.

If you have any questions, please call me to discuss. Again, we seek a peaceful resolution. But, if you do not execute and return to me the enclosed quit claim deed/easement within 20 days, then A.R.S. § 12-1103 will entitle me to an award of attorneys' fees and costs in the quiet title lawsuit that will be filed after the 20-day statutory time period expires.

Very truly yours,

If you file a quiet title action, or any action relating to title to real estate for that matter, you may need to record a "notice of lis pendens," which notifies all third parties that there is a dispute related to title to your property. A notice of lis pendens should be recorded in situations where an adverse title interest could potentially be transferred to a third party. If a notice of lis pendens is recorded, then all future recipients of a title interest to the real estate would be "on notice" of the pending claims, and in most circumstances, will accept any transferred interest in the property subject to the outcome of the quiet title lawsuit.

In other words, if the person filing the lawsuit and recording the notice of lis pendens ultimately wins the litigation, they can obtain "clear" title to property, even if the buyer paid for the property and was unaware of the notice of lis pendens or the underlying quiet title lawsuit. It is because of this that title companies will generally not provide title insurance on properties that have a notice of lis pendens recorded against them.

Pro Tip: Be careful when recording a notice of lis pendens. You may be subjecting yourself to liability under A.R.S. § 33-420 (the statute cited earlier in this chapter). A notice of lis pendens may only be recorded if a lawsuit has been filed and the lawsuit is one "affecting title to real property." Just because you sue a neighbor, or someone else, and you eventually want to record a lien or judgment against their property, this, alone, does not mean the lawsuit affects real property. If you are considering recording a notice of lis pendens, it is important that you understand the potential liability for recording one incorrectly.

• Don't Divert Your Neighbors Water (Or Poison His Dog)

Joe and his wife Suzette lived in the high rent district at the base of a large mountain. Not only did they have a 5,500 square foot home in an exclusive neighborhood that included athletes and politicians, their guest home located toward the southern portion of their 1.5-acre estate consisted of approximately 2,500 livable square feet and was nicer than most homes in "normal" neighborhoods. Their neighbors to the south and a bit lower on the mountain, Dick and Lori, also enjoyed the high life (Dick was the same guy who trespassed by hitting errant golf balls, described in an earlier chapter).

At the southern end of Joe and Suzette's property, there was a masonry block wall separating their property and Dick and Lori's property. The masonry block wall separating the 2 properties contained a wall outlet that permitted the drainage of rain waters and other debris from Joe and Suzette's Property onto Dick and Lori's and elsewhere. This was a design feature required to be constructed due to concerns of flooding and draining.

For several years, Dick and Lori repeatedly placed plywood, mesh, and other debris over the wall outlet to obstruct the natural flow of flood water and debris from Joe and Suzette's property. Dick and Lori also created a landscaping plan that impeded the drainage of rain waters and other debris from Joe and Suzette's property. Basically, they created unnatural mounding near the wall outlet, which had the effect of backing up water onto Joe and Suzette's property and not allowing it to move in its natural way through Dick and Lori's property.

On numerous occasions Joe and Suzette requested that Dick and Lori remove the plywood, mesh, and other debris away from the wall outlet because Joe and Suzette were concerned that this trash would block the natural flow of water and other debris away from their property, as intended by the developers of this neighborhood.

Dick and Lori refused to remove this trash barrier, and despite claiming to be adults, began engaging in threatening behavior (e.g., hitting golf balls onto Joe and Suzette's property; throwing metal grating onto the Joe and Suzette's property in an attempt to harm and agitate Joe and Suzette's dogs; kicking Joe and Suzette's dogs; poking Joe and Suzette's dogs; and of course, planting poisonous vegetation near the drainage outlet and putting peanut butter on the leaves of the poisonous vegetation in an apparent attempt to sicken the Joe and Suzette's dogs). You know, really mature stuff for a couple in their early 50s living the good life.

During a particularly strong mid-September monsoon storm, flood waters inundated Joe and Suzette's property, causing significant "ponding" to their property. And, because Dick and

Lori placed plywood, mesh, and other debris at the wall outlet just prior to the storm, storm water and debris located on Joe and Suzette's property was unable to escape from their yard, as it was engineered to do. This led to water and debris inundating Joe and Suzette's guest home, septic field, outdoor kitchen, landscaping and pool. The wrongful placement of vegetation and mounding near the wall outlet reduced the outlet's flow of water as well, and exacerbated the inundation of flood waters and the ponding of water onto Joe and Suzette's property. In short, the debris and waters were unable to move downstream through the wall outlet as originally designed and intended.

Basically, the guest home was shot, as water levels in the guest home were 3 feet high, ruining the drywall, furniture, and causing a whole host of other issues. All thanks to Dick and Lori wanting to be obnoxious.

Joe and Suzette sent photos and demands for reimbursement of the nearly $600,000 in repair costs to Dick and Lori, who never responded. But, rest assured, a jury of their peers responded, and awarded Joe and Suzette a boatload in damages.

The statute at issue in this neighbor dispute was A.R.S. § 48-3613(A). This statute provides as follows: [A] person shall not engage in any development which will divert, retard or obstruct the flow of waters in any watercourse without securing written authorization from the board of the district in which the watercourse is located.

A.R.S. § 48-3613(D) addresses the remedies provided for a violation of the water diversion statute and allows for an injunction to stop the offending diversion, damages, and/or an award of attorneys' fees and costs. Basically, all that must be shown to recover from someone who has improperly diverted water is: (1) a diversion, retardation, or obstruction of a watercourse; (2) a lack of authorization from the local flood district; and (3) the possibility of resulting damages. Proof of actual damages to someone's home is not required.

Dick and Lori violated this statute and paid dearly for it.

Joe and Suzette similarly recovered under the theories of negligence, trespass, and strict liability. In Arizona, a homeowner is strictly liable for damages resulting from the discharge of storm water onto a neighbor's property.

Pro Tips: Communication is key, if possible. Request that your neighbors stop interfering with the water's path. Sometimes it is too late and before your neighbor can remove their debris or whatever else may be impeding water, the damage has already been done. So, insurance is also key.

Usually, if water comes into your home from a source inside your home – like a broken toilet or a ruptured pipe, your homeowners' insurance company should pick up the claim. If there is a concern that water is coming from outside, or you live in certain designated areas, you may need to obtain flood insurance.

If, however, the problem is caused by a neighbor, like it was for Joe and Suzette, your neighbor's insurance should pick up the damages. And, after paying you, they'll likely cancel your neighbor's insurance policy, like they did to Dick and Lori.

CHAPTER FIVE

Special Types Of Neighbor Issues

"Nothing makes you more tolerant of a neighbor's noisy party than being there."

— *Franklin P. Jones*

• Homeowners' Associations

Mary has owned her home for 15 years and the home is situated within a homeowners' association, i.e., an HOA. The HOA is governed by standard CC&Rs, or Covenants, Conditions & Restrictions (more on CC&Rs below) and is set up to run like a corporation with various committees, meetings, boards, and officers. In her backyard, she has a large eucalyptus tree. Mary's neighbor across her backyard, a man named Paul Meyers, recently became President of Mary's HOA. There is nothing in the governing documents or CC&Rs addressing plants in homeowner's backyards. Early in the year, Mary received a notice from her HOA that she needed to trim her eucalyptus tree – which, again, was in her backyard. Mary, having never reviewed her CC&Rs, nevertheless complied with the HOA's demand.

Mary then received another notice that instructed her to trim her tree and to pay a fine. She trimmed her tree and paid the fine.

She then received another notice and another fine stating that she did not properly pick up the leaves when she trimmed the tree. She was warned that her trimming was inadequate and failure to properly trim her tree would result in the HOA entering her yard to trim the tree for her. She asked that the HOA give her guidance on what was expected and, at a regularly scheduled Board meeting, the Board indicated they wanted to see a properly trimmed tree. The Board also told Mary that it had a preferred list of landscaping vendors and she ought to use one of the preferred vendors if she "wanted to stay out of trouble."

As the Board meeting concluded, Mary walked into the parking lot and sat in her car feeling completely dejected by what just occurred. As she sat in her car contemplating her options, she noticed her neighbor Paul, the new president, climbing into a large Ford truck. Attached to the truck was a trailer full of chainsaws, blowers, and weed-wacker looking things (Mary did not know how to described them when she met with me). With the little sunlight remaining, Mary was able to make out the words "PMs Landscaping Services" plastered on a vinyl wrap on the side of the truck. Mary then realized that "PM," i.e., Paul Meyers, her neighbor and new Board President, was the owner of one of the companies "recommended" by the Board that night. She came to learn that Paul also owned several other landscaping companies in her area.

Sound familiar? Are board members permitted to use their position to promote, or worse, require the use of their services by others in an HOA?

What happens when disgruntled board members take things up a notch and defame other board members or homeowners in the community. It happens all of the time. Take Betty, for example.

Betty was a member on her HOA's Board for many years. She

enjoyed getting to know her neighbors and, over the years, was able to spearhead a number of cost saving endeavors for the HOA.

One of the other Board members, Pete Pivala, lived down the street from Betty in the community. Paul did not like Betty because she voted "No" to using Pete's company to paint several of the community-owned parks. Betty sought to avoid the very issue that Paul Meyers stepped into when he forced, or attempted to force, homeowners in Mary's neighborhood to use his services. Indeed, Betty was well aware of her fiduciary obligations and knew that using Pete could be seen as a major conflict of interest. Besides, Pete's prices were not that great and his Yelp reviews were not that great, either.

And, years of inhaling paint fumes made Pete rather aggressive and dulled his ability to think rationally. Pete's disposition, along with his new dislike of Betty, made the upcoming Board election a rather contentious one. About a week prior to the upcoming Board election, "Painter Pete" (as our firm affectionately called him) canvassed the neighborhood and handed out flyers to homeowners that looked just like actual election ballots. He had access to the ballot forms, as he had been the Board's secretary in prior years, and decided to doctor the forms to ensure himself a victory and another 2 years as a Board member.

Indeed, the ballots displayed by Painter Pete when he canvassed the neighborhood were not real ballots. Rather, the "ballots" were manipulated by Painter Pete to give the impression that Betty was no longer running for a Board position – even though this was untrue. Betty most certainly was running for a position. Pete hacked into the HOA's ballot forms, entered a "strike" line through Betty's name and, at the bottom of the ballot, included a write-in vote for one of Pete's neighbors. Although the ultimate election ballot that homeowners received did not look exactly like Pete's hack job, the damage had been done. Most homeowners were under the misimpression that Betty was no longer interested in a spot on the Board.

The election occurred and Pete was re-elected, as was the write-in candidate. Betty was informed that she received just one vote- her own. She was unaware of the ballot issue until after the election.

If you think Betty was mad, think again. She kept her cool and sued Pete for defamation and prevailed to the tune of $70,000. Defamation is a statement that brings another person into disrepute, or ridicule, or is said to impeach the integrity, virtue, reputation, or honesty of another. Those affected by a defamatory statement made by a neighbor or Board member can sue for damages for emotional distress, monetary loss, or impairment of a reputation.

It happens all of the time, especially whenever an HOA officer, Board member, agent, or employee harms the reputation of a homeowner, or in Betty's case, another Board member. These name-calling episodes usually occur when a Board member is challenged by a homeowner. Board members can get heated with each other, as well, like when the President of a local Board stated the following about another Board member (and neighbor): "I want that bitch thrown in jail, because she is a criminal." This statement made in a public forum, cost the President a cool $25,000 and his spot in an upcoming election.

Oh, I forgot to mention, as a part of Betty's settlement, Pete was forbidden from ever running for a Board position again and, because of his defamatory statements, Pete's own insurance company sued him to recover the money they paid to Betty.

Bizarre HOA voting issues have come up in other neighborly circumstances, too.

Nate knows all too well what happens when CC&Rs give

too much power to other homeowners. Nate purchased vacant land just north of Phoenix. He liked the idea of being away from the city and the land he purchased was beautiful. The land he purchased was approximately 2.5 acres and there were three other properties in the area consisting of similar acreage. Nate planned to construct a single family home, with an RV garage on the land. The property had a brief, but recorded, set of CC&Rs that required the construction of single-family homes of at least 3,400 square feet; and required the vote of 75% of the owners to amend the CC&Rs. The CC&Rs were obviously drafted by one of the other owners in the area, and there was no real substance to them, other than the two requirements already mentioned.

The HOA, which was not an official corporation of any sort and was a loose affiliation of adjacent property owners, consisted of just four members, now including Nate. Three of the 4 members already built their homes. Two of the homes had a north-south orientation, and property adjacent to Nate's property had an east/west orientation. When the owner with the east/west oriented home learned that Nate wanted to position and construct his home with a north/south orientation, he called an immediate meeting to propose a vote to amend the CC&Rs. The vote took place and the existing owners elected to change the CC&Rs to require that the construction and placement of "new homes" were to be in an east/west orientation. This was done to preserve consistency among the homes according to the neighbors (the goal was to have two homes facing north and south and two homes in an east and west orientation). This change only affected Nate because all other homes had been fully constructed.

Ordinarily, the neighbors who ganged up on Nate would have prevailed. They held a valid meeting and held a valid vote. They complied with the CC&Rs. But, Nate actually prevailed here. Because Nate had already obtained a permit to build his home (in fact, he was going to break ground a day after the vote), construction was deemed to have already commenced. As a consequence, the amendment was useless in preventing Nate from continuing to construct his home.

Speaking of construction projects permitted, or not permitted, by an HOA, what happens when an HOA refuses to listen to a homeowner who will be negatively affected by their neighbor's major remodeling project? Just ask Frank.

Frank owned a home adjacent to Brad and both properties were located within a homeowners' association and subject to CC&Rs. The CC&Rs authorized the appointment of a property management company to oversee the operations of the HOA and the enforcement of the CC&Rs. Here, Woodstone Investment Management covered those duties and interpreted and enforce of the CC&Rs for the Board. Well, sort of.

The CC&Rs authorized the creation of an architectural committee to determine the appropriateness of certain improvements for properties within the HOA, including Frank and Brad's properties. According to the CC&Rs, only those improvements and alterations to properties within the HOA that matched the harmony of the design with surrounding structures and topography, were permitted.

And, at least according to an email from Doug Woodstone of Woodstone Investment Management, neither the HOA, nor Woodstone, were even allowed to consider plans to alter the appearance of a home in the neighborhood "without the submitter providing written approval" from the adjoining landowners. In other words, under the CC&Rs and Woodstone's [mis]interpretation of them, the HOA could not consider approving a request from a homeowner to construct, alter, or improve a property within the

HOA unless adjoining landowners first approved that request, in writing.

If you guessed that Brad wanted to construct a monstrous addition to his home, one that would infringe on Frank's mountain views and drastically change the footprint of Brad's home, you would be correct. And, if you also guessed that no plans were ever submitted to neighbors, you would also be correct. And, if you guessed that Brad and the Board met privately on numerous occasions to discuss the significant structural changes to the home and the use of one of the Board member's construction companies to handle most of the work, you're getting really good at this. Frank had no say in anything and did not even know of the project until he awoke to jackhammering early in the morning.

Surely, HOAs were not created to provide unlimited authority to govern neighbors in this fashion. But, these cases are a byproduct of poor documentation, bad management, and a handful of power-hungry neighbors. In legal parlance, an HOA is a private association of homeowners. HOAs are usually formed by a real estate developer for the purpose of marketing, managing, and selling homes and lots in a new residential subdivision.

The first modern planned community was Levittown in New York. This initial planned community still exists on Long Island, and is largely the handiwork of builder William Levitt. Levitt constructed a series of inexpensive homes that veterans could purchase with low-interest loans guaranteed by the federal government under the Servicemen's Readjustment Bill of 1944 (better known as the GI Bill). Between 1947 and 1951 more than 17,000 houses were built in and around the original Long Island community.

While Levittown is credited as being the first planned community, the legal basis for creating such a community came from court sanctioned use of covenants and deed restrictions recorded against certain properties. Oftentimes, these recorded documents were drafted to control the people who could buy in a development, or what could be done to a property. For example, shortly after World War II, many deed restrictions were recorded against properties to exclude African Americans and, in some cases, Jews and Asians, especially on the West Coast. A racial covenant in a Seattle, Washington, neighborhood stated, "No part of said property hereby conveyed shall ever be used or occupied by any Hebrew or by any person of the Ethiopian, Malay or any Asiatic race." And, it was common that these restrictions would have even more offensive language in them. In 1948, the United States Supreme Court ruled such covenants to be unenforceable. However, some private contracts kept them alive until the Fair Housing Act of 1968 prohibited such discrimination.

Thereafter, a number of factors led to a period of rapid growth and popularity of HOAs in the 1960s, including the Fair Housing Act of 1968. Large-scale suburban residential development was encouraged by the Federal Housing Authority and the Urban Land Institute, as the construction of highways had made commuting to cities from outside areas easy. Additionally, there was an increasing social preference to control and preserve architectural quality in developments, which could be easily accomplished through the use of an HOA. As suburban living continued to become a more attractive option, other developments were built, albeit on a smaller scale than Levittown. These developments were often more self-contained than the large-scale communities in that they maintained stricter standards regarding the appearance of the homes (both the structures and the landscaping). The general idea was that people who were looking for certain amenities (whether restrictions on pets or rules governing hedge planting) would be drawn to these communities; those who sought other amenities would look at other developments.

Usually HOAs are structured in one of two ways. They are either private, non-profit corporations or they are unincorporated associations. HOAs are governed by federal and state statutes applicable to corporations (or unincorporated associations if so structured), as well as the HOA's own "governing documents". These governing documents generally "run with the land", which means that all current and future owners of property within the HOA will be bound by them as a condition of property ownership. They usually include:

• CC&Rs: These are usually recorded real property records of the county or other jurisdiction where the subdivision is located. Commonly the CC&Rs specify what types of structures can be placed on a lot and contain other property restrictions.

• The HOA's Articles of Incorporation and Bylaws.

• In some cases the documents may include board-enacted rules as authorized (expressly or implicitly) by the CC&Rs.

Because most HOA's are non-profit corporations, they must follow corporate law and, therefore, are governed by a board of directors. The initial set of board members are developer-appointed members. This ensures that the community continues to be developed with the same characteristics that the original developer created. Once the developer sells the majority of homes, the board's makeup changes such that the board will ultimately consist of homeowner-elected board members. Elections for board membership usually occur every year or two and regular meetings must also occur. Board meetings may be required to be open to the public, except in instances where a board may enter into "executive session" for discussion on confidential, or attorney-client, matters.

The board of directors makes decisions regarding the HOA, including management of the HOA's finances, protecting the HOA's real and intangible assets (generally the amenities provided which were the basis for inducing people to purchase lots), and enforcing the governing documents. Boards of directors have a fiduciary duty to the property owners; violation of that duty may result in liability for individual directors.

HOA governing documents often provide broad authority to their boards. Depending on the governing documents, HOA boards may create committees, such as an "architectural control committee." Additionally, depending on the governing documents and state law, the HOA may have the authority to place liens on a property and to, ultimately, foreclose on it. The major power of the HOA and a board, however, is the ability to compel property owners to pay a share of common expenses for the overall maintenance of the HOA and the amenities, usually proportionate to their ownership interests (either by unit or based on square footage).

Pro Tips:

1. Board members have fiduciary obligations to property owners within the HOA, and breach of fiduciary duty is a common claim alleged against board members. The two primary fiduciary duties are the duty of care, and the duty of loyalty. The duty of care requires board members to act on an informed basis after due consideration of all information. The duty of loyalty requires

board members to look to the interests of the community and not to their personal interests. Failure to enforce a rule contained in the CC&Rs or elsewhere may give rise to a breach of fiduciary duty claim.

2. You have the right to challenge your HOA if they are trying to collect more than they are entitled to collect and to have a hearing for any alleged HOA violation.

3. You should read your CC&Rs, bylaws, and other governing documents before purchasing, or making improvements to your home. You do not want to give your neighbor any ammunition to argue that your improvements violate the CC&Rs.

4. You and your neighbors have the right to petition to remove directors from the board. In communities with 1,000 members or fewer, the process for removal is triggered if the board receives a petition signed by people entitled to cast 25% of the votes, or 100 votes, whichever is less. In communities with over 1,000 members, the process is triggered if the board receives a petition signed by people entitled to cast 10% of the votes, or 1,000 votes, whichever is less.

5. Generally, the CC&Rs are enforceable as a contract between a homeowner and the HOA and as a contract among homeowners. This means that even if an HOA refuses to enforce regulations imposed by the CC&Rs, individual homeowners can enforce them.

6. If you think that your HOA or your neighbors, with the assistance of your HOA, are ganging up on you, you're probably correct. You have the right to inspect the records of an HOA.

Here is a "form" letter for requesting information:

REQUEST TO REVIEW/INSPECT
ASSOCIATION RECORDS

MAIL TO: _____Homeowners
Association

Name of Owner/Member or designated representative making
request: _____
    Address and lot/unit number: _____
    Phone number(s): _____
    I request to review/inspect the following records of the
Association (please check below records).
    _____I prefer to come by the Association/Management
office on _____, 20__,   at (__)m or another convenient day.
    _____I prefer to have documents mailed to me with
all appropriate copy and mailing costs being placed on my
account (Please see below).
- -
- -
    _____Membership list with addresses (without
Phone Numbers)
    _____(initials) I avow that I
    -will not use the list or any part for any purpose unrelated
to a Member's interest as a member
    -will not use it to solicit money or property
    -will not use it for any commercial purpose
    -will not sell it to any person
    -MUST CHOOSE ONE OF THE FOLLOWING
    will use it solely for the purpose of communication with
other Members for a scheduled membership meeting on

_____OR will use it for the following proper purpose described with reasonable particularity (use must be directly connected to the stated purpose):

_____ Other records requiring showing of proper purpose:

_____Accounting records (specify):

_____(Initials) I avow that I will use them for the following proper purpose described with reasonable particularity (use must be directly connected to the stated purpose): _____.

_____Most recent financial statements

_____(Initials) I avow that I will use them for the following proper purpose described with reasonable particularity (use must be directly connected to the stated purpose): _____

_____ Minutes of Board meeting for _____.

_____ Record of Board action without meeting (i.e., unanimous consent), related to _____.

_____ Minutes of Membership meetings older than three years (specify years) _____

_____.

_____Records of Committee actions related to: _____

_____

_____ (Initials) I avow that I will use these records for the following proper purpose described with reasonable particularity (use must be directly connected to the stated purpose):

_____.

Other Documents (purpose not required)
_____Articles of Incorporation

_____Bylaws

_____Board Resolutions relating to Member rights and obligations

_____Minutes of Members' meetings and records of action taken without a meeting (past three years). Specify year

_____Written communications to the Members for past three years, including financial statements (except proper purpose needed for the latter)

_____List of names and business addresses of current directors and officers

_____List of names and addresses of Members of the Association

_____Most recent corporate annual report

_____Any other specific record(s) of the Association, as listed below:

CONSENT

I hereby acknowledge that the Association will charge me $.15 per page for copies of any and all documents to which I request copies. If I wish documents to be mailed to me, I acknowledge that the Association will charge applicable mailing costs to my account.

Date _____, 20__   _____

• 'Lil Devil, his Adult Videos, and his Short Term Rentals

"Look at this, MacQueen," shouted Steve, the owner of a high-end home in Paradise Valley, as we sat in my office. "Uh, Steve, I think you meant to show me something different. Why are you showing me a porno video?" Because, as Steve so bluntly put it "that's my GD house in the background, that's my window, that's my trellis, those are my palm trees, that's my bougainvillea, and that's the side of my garage, and those three people are having sex on the pool deck of my neighbors' home." OK, I replied, as I contemplated what could possibly be done about the situation.

And, "this" said Steve, "look at this!" He handed me his phone again and showed me a rap video, with what I now knew to be his "GD house" and bougainvillea plants in the background.

"Well, Steve," I replied, "what would you like me to do about it? And, candidly, how did you find these videos?" Steve then explained that, about a month ago, he heard a bunch of commotion at the home directly to his west and so he went to the home and asked a man walking from the front door to a car parked in the driveway about what was going on. In response, the man looked at Steve strangely and asked, "Do you know who 'Lil Devil is?" Steve shook his head no, and then received a card from the man as he entered his car. As it turned out, Steve was speaking with the producer of adult films and music videos, who had been renting Steve's neighbor's home periodically as a short term rental to party and make videos. Steve later found the videos on the internet.

Rap and adult videos and his house featured in them triggered Steve into becoming an expert on short term rentals, VRBOs, and Airbnbs, and also led to his filing of a claim for nuisance against his neighbor. It also led him to contacting various state legislators to try to change the current status of the law in his state.

Short term rentals are of increasing concern to homeowners and can put strain on the relationships between neighbors. On the one hand, owning property comes with a "bundle of rights," including the opportunity to rent property to another individual and to make money doing so. But, advancing technology, including Al Gore's 1995 creation of the internet, has expanded choices for consumer travel and changed the traditional rental market time frames to much shorter periods.

Other sources of strain are the difficulty in balancing rights to earn money and the negative effects if a neighbor is renting their home as a "party house." If you're against short term rentals, the bad news is that there's evidence that platforms such as VRBO and Airbnb have now become an accepted way to book a vacation. The good news is that in areas where short term rentals are accepted or encouraged, your neighbor's use of a home as a vacation rental may result in raising the value of your home.

While you may believe that your neighbor's use of his home as a short term rental is a new phenomenon, it is not. And, the history of using a residence as a vacation, or short term rental, shows that these uses are not going away.

These uses date back as far as the mid-1600s, and researchers believe the first vacation rental property was none other than Louis XIV's Palace of Versailles. The Palace of Versailles was first built as a hunting lodge for Louis XIII. Successor Louis XIV expanded the lodge into the palace we know today. This palace actually became a spot for entreating various political heads and for the buddies of Louis to drink French wine and hunt.

Later in the 1600s, the Apostolic Palace of Castel Gandolfo in Italy was constructed. For centuries, it has been used as a place for the Pope to vacation.

Fast forward a couple hundred years and sail northwest from France, i.e., to the English countryside, where researchers found letters from friends asking friends to use vacation homes via snail mail and waiting weeks for a response. Around this same time, large, wealthy families began investing in vacation homes and sharing them through various ownership structures.

In the 1950s, vacation rentals begin to appear in U.S. newspapers and real estate agent begin touting the ability to use vacation homes for rental purposes.

In 1995, when Al Gore, "took the initiative to create the Internet," another creation was born: Vacation Rentals by Owner (or, VRBO). VRBO initially consisted of one listing for a property in Breckenridge, Colorado. Ten years later, HomeAway launched as a merger of five different vacation rental sites and HomeAway subsequently purchased VRBO, and its inventory of listed vacation rentals reached several hundred thousand.

Airbnb, on the other hand, began listing properties in 2008 as a way for owners to rent out rooms in their homes. The impetus for the creation of Airbnb was the lack of hotel rooms near convention centers.

By 2015, the vacation rental industry was worth more than $85 billion, and HomeAway alone, has more than 2.8 million rooms available – more rooms than the four largest hotel chains in the world. And, the average homeowner utilizing their home for vacation rental purposes is earning nearly $30,000 in annual revenue.

Short term rentals aren't going anywhere.

Pro Tips:

If you are a homeowner negatively affected by short term rentals in your neighborhood, try an informal conversation with your neighbor addressing your concerns. If that does not work, you may discover that your neighbor's use of their home as a short term or vacation rental violates local code, and your next step would be to report the violation to local officials. For example, homes available for rental in Scottsdale are permitted to have a maximum family size of six adults (and their related dependent children). This code violation occurs every night in many parts of Scottsdale.

Even if there are no code violations, you may have a claim that your neighbor has created a nuisance, thereby entitling you to money damages.

Another option is to sift through any deed restrictions or CC&Rs affecting the home to determine if any violation of those documents exist. Many CC&Rs prohibit rentals of less than 30 days, and many deed restrictions prohibit the use of homes as businesses.

Yet another option is to seek an injunction - a court order that the renting must stop for a certain amount of time.

If you are a homeowner that opens your home to short term guests, be a good neighbor. Communicate with your neighbors about the use of your home, provide neighbors with your contact information or that of your property manager. Assure your neighbors that short term rentals may actually increase the value of homes in the neighborhood. Specifically, the homes available for short term use are usually cleaner than most homes in the neighborhood due to the mandatory cleaning after guests depart, the curb appeal is usually higher, and the homes being utilized as short term rentals are often more up to date, as owners need to stay competitive with other homeowners in the area using their homes as rentals. And, of course, follow up with your neighbors as to whether any issues occur.

Additionally, assure your neighbors that you have created "house rules" that you expect guests to follow, and have these rules include: quiet hours; no visitors past a certain time; no smoking; a parking policy; instructions on pool, spa, and fireplace usage; and that the home is limited to those on the guest application. You may take things one step further and install noise monitoring devices to further assure neighbors that noise levels are monitored, and/or hiring a security guard to roam the area.

As an aside, if you use your home for short term rental income and have confirmed that there are no deed restrictions or HOA rules that prohibit such use, be sure to create an entity, like a limited liability company to own the property, obtain the correct property insurance, and create an agreement for the use of your home that addresses the rules outlined above.

The Arizona legislature created some of the "friendliest" rules when it comes to short term and vacation rentals. The only rules of much significance require an owner to obtain a transaction privilege tax license and display the license number in any home listings, and to provide contact information to local authorities. That's it. But, as an owner of a short term rental, you should definitely continue to monitor the laws, as they are very much in flux.

CONCLUSION

"He who throws mud only loses ground"

— Fat Albert

There is an incredible upside to owning real estate. As they say, real estate appreciates over time, owning real estate provides for unique tax benefits, real estate investing can provide steady cash flow, and owning real estate allows for leveraging and building equity.

But, there are a number of Bernies, Darrens and Rons out there. And, more often than not, there are the honorable, sincere, fair, and law-abiding neighbors that find themselves being denied their peaceful, quiet, and enjoyable use of their property. Why? It is usually because it is the honest, trusting neighbors that wait the longest to learn how real estate laws work. These are the neighbors who do everything that their neighbors, or their HOA, ask or require of them, often not realizing that their trust is misplaced. They often start with no intention of learning about real estate laws, or even consider hiring an attorney or filing a lawsuit, and they often suffer greatly as a result of this otherwise admirable mentality.

If these honest neighbors knew how real estate laws worked and understood the historical underpinnings for the laws, these well-intentioned folks could increase the likelihood of a favorable outcome, or at least a fair settlement. If they were provided valuable information and warned of potential pitfalls involving real estate laws, they would undoubtedly increase the chances of a fair result for their situation.

Real estate laws should not be a secret, something that only attorneys, judges, and experienced real estate agents should have access to. This book does not replace the need to consult with, and potentially hire, a real estate attorney. But, hopefully, this book can help inform you when making the decision as to whether a real estate attorney is necessary. And hopefully you now understand some of the hurdles that you may face, and the mistakes that may be made, when dealing with a difficult neighbor.

A SPECIAL OFFER FOR YOU

Let's say you're dealing with a nasty neighbor. Your goal is to inexpensively resolve the issue without the need for a lawyer. But, there's just one problem: you don't have any of the forms or letters or documents that you need to for a successful resolution. And, you do not want to recreate the wheel by drafting something that might not work. So, what can you do?

Over the course of my 16-year career, I've accumulated numerous forms, letters, and documents to assist in dealing with a difficult neighbor. You can have these documents by asking for them. Just give me a call at **480-433-3481** or email me at **Patrick@mandglawgroup.com** and let me know what you need. No strings attached!

HELPFUL REAL ESTATE DEFINITIONS

I often see homeowners, real estate agents, and yes, other real estate attorneys, goofing up the understanding of words used in the real estate world and not using the proper terminology when addressing and analyzing the common neighbor disputes described in this book. But, before defining various words, I would be remiss if I didn't point out two of the most commonly misused words in the legal and real estate worlds. First, the words "mute" and "moot." There is no such thing as a "mute" point. Rather, it is a "moot" point, which means that the argument or issue being addressed is of no significance. Second, the pronunciation of the word "realtor" is often mispronounced as a "real-uh-tor" or "real-a-tor." The word "realtor" has two syllables – not 3. If you have been mispronouncing the word, like I did for about a year, try to pronounce the word as follows: "real-tore." Hopefully this helps.

amortization
The breakdown of your loan payments over time. Your loan payment consists of a portion which will be applied to pay the accruing interest on a loan, with the remainder being applied to the principal. Over time, the interest portion decreases as the loan balance decreases, and the amount applied to principal increases so that the loan is paid off (amortized) in the specified time – typically 15 or 30 years for a traditional home loan.

appraisal

A written justification of the price to be paid for a property, which is usually based on an analysis of sales of comparable properties nearby.

appreciation

The increase in the value of a property due to changes in market conditions, inflation, or other factors.

assessed value

The valuation placed on property by a local tax assessor for purposes of taxation.

assessor

A public official who establishes the value of a property for taxation purposes.

as-is

A provision in a contract that indicates that the property is being sold in its existing physical condition.

balloon mortgage

A loan that requires the remaining principal balance be paid at a specific point in time. For example, a loan may be amortized as if it would be paid over a thirty-year period, but requires that at the end of the 5th year, the entire balance must be paid in full.

balloon payment

The final lump sum payment that is due at the end of a balloon mortgage.

broker

Most real estate "brokers" are actually real estate "agents" who work under a "broker." Some agents can be brokers as well, either working for themselves or under another broker.

chain of title

A review of transfers of title to a piece of property.

clear title

A title that is free of liens or issues regarding the ownership of property.

cloud on title or clouded title

Conditions revealed by a title report that adversely affect the title to real estate that may need to be removed.

collateral

For a real estate loan, i.e., a loan to purchase a home, the property is the collateral. The borrower risks losing the property if the loan is not repaid.

common areas

Those portions of a building, land, and/or amenities owned by a planned unit development or condominium project's homeowners' association that are used by all of the unit owners, who share in the expenses of their operation and maintenance. For instances, common areas include swimming pools, tennis courts, and other recreational facilities, as well as hallways, parking areas and streets.

common law
A body of law based on general custom, or case precedence, that began in England.

condominium
A type of ownership in real property in which all of the owners own the property, common areas and buildings together, with the exception of the interior of a unit, which an owner has actual title to.

Covenants, conditions, and restrictions ("CC&Rs")
An enforceable contract recorded against title to property, that may limit or restrict certain uses of the property.

deed of trust
Lenders in some states, like Arizona, typically use deeds of trust as security for real estate loans, instead of a mortgage.

due-on-sale provision
A provision in a deed of trust that allows the lender to demand repayment in full if the borrower sells, or transfers, the property.

earnest money deposit
A deposit made by the potential purchaser of real estate to prove that the purchaser intends to purchase the property.

easement
A property right giving persons other than the owner access to or over a property.

eminent domain
The right of a government to take private property for public use

upon payment of its fair market value to the property owner.

encroachment

Something, e.g., a building, fence, etc., that intrudes on another's property.

encumbrance

Something that restricts or limits free use of a property, like a lease, easement, or other restriction.

fee simple

The greatest possible interest a person can have in real estate.

fixture

Personal property that becomes real property when attached in a permanent manner to real estate. For instance, "custom" bookshelves or a pergola.

flood insurance

Insurance that compensates for physical property damage resulting from flooding. It is required in order to obtain a real estate loan on properties located in federally designated flood areas.

foreclosure

The process by which a borrower in default under a mortgage or deed of trust loses their property.

grantee

The person to whom an interest in real estate is conveyed, e.g., a buyer.

grantor
The person conveying an interest in real property, e.g., a seller.

homeowners' association
A nonprofit association that manages the common areas of a planned unit development or condominium project.

joint tenancy
A form of ownership or taking title to property which means each party owns the entire property. In the event of the death of one party, the survivor owns the property in its entirety.

judgment
A decision made by a court of law and oftentimes recorded in the real property records.

lease
An agreement between the property owner, as the landlord, and a tenant that provides an interest in real estate to the tenant for a specific period of time, so long as the tenant satisfies payment and other conditions of the lease.

lease option
An alternative financing option that allows home buyers to lease a home with an option to purchase it at a later date. Each month's rent payment may consist of rent and an additional amount credited toward the ultimate purchase price for the property.

legal description
A property description, recognized by law, that provides the specific location and identity of real property.

lien

A legal claim against title to a property. A deed of trust deed is considered a lien.

mortgage

A legal document that pledges a property to the lender as security for payment of a debt. Instead of mortgages, some states utilize deeds of trust.

mortgagee (or "beneficiary" if a deed of trust is used)

The lender in a mortgage agreement.

mortgagor (or "borrower" if a deed of trust is used)

The borrower in a mortgage agreement.

note a.k.a. "promissory note"

A legal promise that a borrower repay a loan.

power of attorney

A legal document that authorizes another person to act on one's behalf, which may include the ability to purchase or sell real estate on someone else's behalf.

quitclaim deed

A deed that transfers title to real estate without warranty. Such a deed conveys title that a grantor may have at the time the conveyance is made.

Real Estate Settlement Procedures Act (RESPA)

A consumer protection law that requires lenders to give borrowers advance notice of closing costs, among other things.

recorder
The public official who keeps records of transactions that affect real estate.

recording
The act of noting in the registrar's office certain details of a property transaction, which can include providing notice of the existence of a deed, a deed of trust, judgment, or the "release" of a document, thereby putting third parties "on notice" of the existence of the document.

rights of ingress or egress
The legal right to enter or leave/exit certain real estate.

seller carry-back
An agreement in which the owner of a property provides financing, often in combination with a note and deed of trust in favor of the seller.

subdivision
A real estate development that is created by dividing tracts of land into individual lots for sale.

survey
A drawing or map showing the legal boundaries of real estate and the location of improvements, encroachments, streets, and other physical features of a property.

title
A person's right to or ownership of a property.

title insurance

Insurance that provides certain insurance coverage for a lender or an owner of real estate against loss associated with a title related dispute or "defects" in title.

title search

A review of title records to determine whether or not certain conditions exist. For example, an owner might request a title search to determine if anyone has placed a lien on title to their home.

ABOUT THE AUTHOR

Patrick MacQueen graduated from Michigan State University with honors and graduated number one at the University of Detroit Mercy School of Law. He practices in the areas of real estate transactions and real estate litigation. Patrick has been selected to the Southwest Super Lawyers Rising Stars list for seven consecutive years. Each year, no more than 2.5 % of the lawyers in the State of Arizona are selected by the research team at Super Lawyers to receive this honor.

In 2019 & 2020, Patrick was selected as a Top 100 Attorney in Arizona by AZ Business Magazine. He also was the recipient of America's Top 100 Attorneys Lifetime Achievement Award – less than one-half percent (0.5%) of active attorneys in the United States will receive this honor. Patrick was also selected as one of the "People to Know in Commercial Real Estate Professionals" for 2020. People & Projects to Know (PTK) is an annual magazine that spotlights Arizona's most influential commercial real estate professionals and the projects that define the landscape. The 2020 Arizona Business Leaders Magazine also featured Patrick. This annual publication profiles the business leaders and innovators that are changing the face of Arizona business.

You can also find Patrick teaching, as he is a highly requested Arizona Department of Real Estate approved instructor, and playing golf, as Patrick is a competitive amateur golfer maintaining a "scratch" handicap. Patrick resides with his family in Phoenix, Arizona.

Made in the USA
Coppell, TX
08 October 2021